reading this.
Best Wishes
Stephen
7/11/19

THE BATTLES FOUGHT

STEPHEN BRIDGE

Former Chief Executive at Papworth, the renowned NHS Hospital

Printed in the United Kingdom

ISBN - 978-1-9160408-0-9

Cover design and layout by www.spiffingcovers.com

Acknowledgements

Many people have commented on the family atmosphere that existed at Papworth Hospital . The staff always "went that extra mile" to ensure that the patients received the very highest quality of care , despite the sub standard conditions of many of the wards. My working relationship with the staff was excellent, and although most of them do not feature in this book, I have wonderful memories of the many things we achieved together over the 28 years at this great hospital.

Probably my closest colleague amongst the consultant medical staff was David Stone, who provided me with sound advice for many years during which he undertook several roles in the management of Papworth. An avid Bob Dylan fan, David educated me to appreciate this great man's work, for which I can't thank him enough.

For the first half of my tenure I was pretty "hands on", a benign autocrat, I was often called, but as the hospital got bigger we needed to appoint a Director of Operations. Claire Tripp carried out this role with distinction for ten years, and also took on a great deal of extra work to design the new Papworth Hospital. Sadly

Claire died in 2017, so was not able to see fruits of her hard earned labour, with the opening of new Papworth Hospital.

Last, but not least, I should like to thank Barbara Gamble , my secretary/personal assistant for my whole time at Papworth.If anyone epitomised the spirit of Papworth, then it was Barbara, who worked so hard, was always polite and courteous in even the most trying of circumstances, and was incredibly loyal to me and the two chairmen she also “tried to keep in order”, Audrey Stenner and John Beadsmoore.

CHAPTER ONE
1974

Good Evening, I'm from Essex

In October 1974, having passed my A levels at the Gilberd School in Colchester, Essex, I made the long journey in my battered Volkswagen to Lancaster University where I was to study for a politics degree. I shared a room with Colin King, who came from Knotty Ash, Liverpool, which until then I had assumed was a figment of Ken Dodd's imagination. It was only the second week when I realised that I had made a bad decision, as the content of the course was too abstract for my liking, and I realised I was homesick. So I returned to Essex, and considered whether I wanted to study for a degree the following year, or take up the offer of working in the City of London.

This offer had been made to me several months earlier by a Lloyd's underwriter and acquaintance of my father. The underwriter, Mr Landon, would call in for a drink on his way home at the same pub which my father used, and owned a second-hand Porsche, which my father had helped him purchase. My father was a car mechanic, working for the local VW garage, and had to supplement his meagre income by servicing cars at the weekends, including a VW Beetle owned by Mr Landon.

I decided against working in London, mainly because of pride: I wanted to get a job based on my own merit, and not accept a favour, however kind the intention was. Instead I applied to join the NHS via their A level entry scheme. Alas, I was not invited for interview, so set about finding a job using the local newspaper. In the meantime, I took a series of temporary positions, including driving a white van, delivering cases of wine for the renowned local firm Lay and Wheeler, before signing on the dole at the local 'labour exchange'.

After only one week I was interviewed for a job at Ipswich Borough Council as a personnel and management services trainee. I was offered the post, and started on 3rd March 1975 on a salary of £1400 – approximately £11,600 circa 2019. I soon found out that the role had very little to do with personnel management, my preferred avenue; instead I was to work in 'Time and Motion', armed with a clipboard and stopwatch, and check the bonus schemes of the council's carpenters, groundsmen and refuse collectors. We were viewed with distaste by most of the staff we met, as our job was associated with job cuts and redundancies by the heavily unionised workforce.

This job also gave me my first insight into how the 'market economy' worked at grass roots-level, as during a study of refuse collectors, I saw first-hand how a little bit of extra service provided by the refuse men – for example, removing rubbish they were not obliged to – was rewarded by a gift of pornographic magazines, or cans of beer, from the grateful shop owner.

The culture of taking a few liberties was also present in my council department, where it was custom and practice to pop out mid-afternoon for a haircut. When I asked why they could not get it done during the lunch hour, the reply was, "It grows on work's time, so it gets cut on work's time."

Enough said!

The highlight of 1975 was our lads' holiday to Torquay where, in Tiffany's Disco, I met a lovely girl, Natalie, from Herefordshire. Our holiday romance could not survive the long distance separating our hometowns, so we opted to become 'pen pals', that quaint old tradition of exchanging letters on a regular basis. After a few months, Natalie told me she was off to live in Houston, Texas, as the company she worked for had recently set up an office there.

After 14 months working in this hostile environment, I was informed by an ex-colleague at the council, Peter Kelly, of three vacancies in the local NHS Time and Motion office, where he now worked. I applied, was successful, and joined the NHS in April 1976, and thankfully consigned my stopwatch to the waste bin as Peter said they used more sophisticated methods to measure efficiency.

The team I joined in Ipswich was an outpost of the Regional Health Authority (RHA) based in Cambridge.

We hardly saw our regional bosses, Arthur and Tony, which gave our team leader, John Halliday, plenty of scope to slip off early and indulge in his real passion of leading a pop music band. The team employed 13 staff, including Maisie, who as John's personal assistant usually managed to do our typing . . . in between her other clerical duties on behalf of her Brownie pack and the Waldringfield Sailing Club.

During my second week in this job, I visited the Cambridge headquarters of the RHA, where Arthur, a lovely man in his late 50s, gave me a tour of the building, including the senior management offices where, unbeknown to me, I was to visit 15 years later, when I was to find out if my hitherto impressive career rise was about to be halted.

I told Arthur that I was off to London that evening to see David Bowie in his Thin White Duke Tour, and he very kindly truncated his official induction talk and gave me a lift to the station.

Over the next couple of years, during Arthur's visit to our Ipswich base, we always made sure there were several copies of adult entertainment magazines for him to peruse in the tea room, where his distinctive northern accent would be heard saying, "Bloody hell, look at that!"

Maisie had a pretty young assistant called Stephanie, and after two months of starting, she and I became an item, winning her affection by buying her two Leonard Cohen long-playing records. In the autumn, Stephanie took the surprising decision to leave damp, foggy Suffolk and move to hot sunny Texas, with her mother and step-father, a pilot in the US Air Force. *Damn it,* I thought, *what is it with me and girlfriends emigrating to Texas.*

One other larger-than-life colleague was Gerry, who hailed from Oldham. He invited me to join him and his mates for a Friday night drink at the Greyhound pub, opposite the Anglesea Road wing of Ipswich Hospital. At one of these sessions, Gerry told me he was going on a secret mission and, outside in the car park, he proceeded to blacken his face with shoe polish, and drove off into the night, promising to tell me all when we were back at work on Monday. Well, he turned up in the office battered and bruised, with several nasty scratches on his face. He had gone to a fish farm, and carefully navigated his way through a thick hedge of hawthorn bushes, taking at least 15 minutes, and then 'liberated' several koi carp to add to his collection at home. Just as he was about to return to his car, he was spotted by the geese which the owners kept as guard animals, so he had little choice but to dash through the hawthorn bushes, in a matter of seconds, narrowly evading the marauding geese.

He invited me to see his new fish, but said it would have to be in a few weeks' time, since he told his wife he got the cuts defending me in a fight at the Greyhound pub, and that I too had sustained two black eyes!

After two years of carrying out routine studies, checking the bonus schemes of catering, cleaning and portering staff in local hospitals, I was given the challenging task of reviewing the bonus scheme for three drivers delivering clean linen to all the outlying hospitals in the eastern part of Suffolk. All three drivers held senior positions in the local branches of the trade unions: the Confederation of Health Service Employees and the Transport and General Workers' Union. I soon discovered the con they had pulled on a predecessor of mine, resulting in them sharing weekly fixed overtime of 33 hours, on top of their bonus payments. I decided to meet them informally in the hospital social club and, over a couple of pints of Abbot Ale, came to a compromise, and reduced their overtime perk to 11 hours per week.

In the fraught industrial relations climate of the time, my ability to deliver a win-win for management and unions was complimented by my boss, who gave me a promotion and told me that I was to be given another delicate assignment. The Callaghan (Labour) government had recently struck a deal with the public service trade unions that required all future bonus schemes to be self-funding, largely to be achieved by reducing the numbers of staff employed by natural wastage.

My task was to introduce self-funding bonus schemes into the four small geriatric hospitals in East Suffolk. These four hospitals were managed by 'old school' hospital administrators, none more so than Stow Lodge, the hospital in Stowmarket. The administrator was Walter Gallon – an apt name, as he kept a bottle of whisky in the bottom drawer of his filing cabinet. Walter was a long-serving NHS person, who had previously been in the Royal Navy, and I quickly deduced that it would be sensible to engage with him on his terms and not offend him by refusing to share a 'wee dram' with this convivial Scotsman.

At another of these four hospitals I was asked if I could avoid going there on a Thursday, as this was the day that a senior member of the Health Authority, based in Ipswich, arranged his 'assignation' with a female member of the hospital staff. The person telling me this said that the hospital enjoyed some minor perks from this liaison, such as better office equipment etc., and they did not want me to disrupt this cosy arrangement.

Music was important to me, and I always listened to the late night John Peel show on my car radio during the long drive back to Ipswich, following a late shift. This is when I first heard 'Anarchy in the UK' by The Sex Pistols, 'White Riot' by The Clash, 'Teenage Kicks' by The Undertones, and the fabulous Ian Dury and the Blockheads, signalling the dawn of punk rock, so important to this day for many of my generation.

Music was also a main topic of our elongated tea breaks in our Ipswich office, especially when Dave, a colleague who started on the same day as me, divulged that he was the keyboard player on the Chicory Tip number one song, 'Son of my Father', a few years earlier. We assumed he was bullshitting, as he never explained why he swapped the glamourous life for standing in a hospital kitchen for eight hours assessing how efficient the dozen or staff were, whom we were observing!

In May 1979, halfway through this 18-month programme at the four hospitals, I bought a one-bedroom flat in a village two miles west of Ipswich. Three months later, in August, I was injured when the car I was a passenger in went into a ditch in a country lane. The driver, Colin, and I were admitted to hospital, he with some broken ribs, and me with a fractured cheek bone and cuts to my face. The several pints of Abbot Ale I had consumed eased the discomfort of having 12 stitches in my forehead, and the three days I spent in hospital recovering from the operation on my cheek, was, under the circumstances, quite pleasant.

I asked one of the nurses on my ward out for a drink, which turned into a pleasant three-month relationship, made the more enjoyable by the £750 payment I received from Colin's insurance company for pain and suffering. It was his suggestion that I made the claim, and as a thank you to him, I spent the next year selling suits, jeans and sweatshirts, imported from Poland and Hungary, for his discount clothes business.

My last shift of the four-hospital programme was to be at Blythburgh Hospital near Southwold, between the hours of 6am and 11am on a Saturday morning in October 1979. For a variety of reasons, it was an event that I remember vividly almost 40 years later. The previous evening, I saw one of the best punk rock bands around when The Ramones played a storming set at Essex University, Colchester. They finished at 11pm, after which I drove to Ipswich and joined my girlfriend's party in the residential accommodation for nursing staff. At 4am, having taken care not to have had any alcoholic drinks, I set off for my 6am start at Blythburgh. The cook who came on duty was, in today's term, transgender, and wore high heels and dangly earrings. Despite my initial surprise, the two of us developed a good repartee and the time passed quickly, until I left at 11am for the 60-mile drive back to Colchester. I played centre half for the Eastern Gas football team, but my lack of sleep caught up with me and we were thrashed 6–0 by the opposition.

My small team spent an enjoyable 18 months designing and installing bonus schemes for the ancillary staff at these four hospitals. The period concluded with some tense, heavy negotiations with the National Union of Public Employees' regional officer, Eddie Braden, a blunt Geordie whose reputation for hard bargaining was legendary. Although I did not realise it at the time, my tough negotiations with the union representatives over those past four years provided me with excellent experience which I was able to call upon in my future NHS career.

As my fourth anniversary of working at the Suffolk Area Management Services Unit approached, I felt that I wanted to work in other areas of NHS management, and prove to myself that I could survive in an environment without the long tea breaks and the Friday 'POETS' culture in the local pub[1].

---

[1] 'Piss off early; tomorrow's Saturday'!

I was successful at my first attempt to find a new job and, in June 1980, gained promotion to become planning officer at the Chelmsford Health District, one of five units of management reporting to the Essex Area Health Authority.

CHAPTER TWO

1980-84

Working in Chelmsford, Jokingly Called 'A Cemetery with Lights'

This job had three components, all of which provided me with valuable experience I would call upon many times over the next 30 years. First, was the compilation of an annual business plan; second, the design and commissioning of hospital buildings; and third, minute secretary to the district management team.

As the new job entailed a daily commute of an 80-mile round trip, I replaced my battered Ford Cortina with a five-year-old shiny yellow Audi 80GT. Unfortunately, the economic recession meant that it was difficult for me to sell my flat in Ipswich, and I was deemed to be too senior to be given a room in the hospital residential accommodation/nurses home in Chelmsford. The NHS rules at that time only reimbursed daily travelling expenses for married staff, and the 12 months it took to sell my flat at a discounted rate ate up all the salary increase I earned in this first year.

In June 1981, I bought a three-bedroom semi-detached house in Chelmsford, and to help pay the big mortgage I took in two lodgers. The first lad to move in had just left home, for the first time, and asked if he could bring his pet bird with him. I stupidly did not ask for details about the bird, and said yes. Two days after he moved in, I returned home at lunchtime and noticed that my tins of paint had been removed from the shed and placed on the garden path. Upon opening the shed door I was greeted by the sight of a two-foot-high buzzard, tethered to a big log, flapping its wings and eating a dead mouse!

Ten minutes later, my neighbour Ron came to see me and said that, although I seemed like a nice bloke, a bird of prey next door was a step too far – he feared for the safety of his pet rabbits.

When I told my lodger that evening to get rid of the buzzard, and the dead mice in the freezer, he took it back to his parent's house, where he followed a week later.

At work, two senior managers ran the show, allowing the district administrator plenty of time to attend endless meetings at the Area Health Authority, held by most to be an unnecessary tier of NHS management, abolished in 1982, only eight years after they were established.

One of these two senior managers was Bob Booker, the finance director, with whom I would spend hours discussing our love of rock music. Rumour had it that Bob did a mean impression of Elvis Presley at his department's Christmas party.

The other manager who called the shots was my boss, Harry Child. Harry was delightfully innocent when it came to affairs of the heart, and could not understand why his devoted secretary would sometimes return late from her lunch break looking flushed. After I got to know her, she confided that she was seeing a married man for a weekly assignation. I offered her the use of my house, and she thanked me by giving me several tins of paint, courtesy of her man, who was a director of a local builder's merchant.

Harry gave me a couple of near-impossible tasks, I suspect to see how I would cope under pressure. The first was to obtain financial damages from Essex County Cricket Club, for breaking windows in the adjoining Chelmsford and Essex Hospital, when a batsman hit a six. Bearing in mind that this was at the time when Graham Gooch was at the height of his powers, the breaking of windows in the hospital kitchen and the pathology laboratory was a pretty frequent event. My request was dismissed out of hand as being 'just one of those things, dear boy'. I then discovered that most of the senior doctors at the hospital had been given free membership of the club, hence silencing any criticism from the most powerful group in the NHS, at that time.

My second 'mission impossible' was to sort out the car parking problems at the same hospital. My genius plan consisted of introducing a one-way system, and allocating parking permits, at £20 a year, for the consultant medical staff. Following my presentation at the consultants' monthly meeting, the proposals were ripped to shreds, with some comments claiming that it 'breached their rights to park wherever they wanted'.

After the meeting, the chairman of the consultants, Dr Hugh James Galbraith, somebody I knew well through his membership of the district management team, which I was secretary of, explained to me that my ideas were sound, but a bit ahead of their time. His comments took me back a few years to exactly the same conversation I'd had with the trade union officials in Ipswich. Although at different ends of the work and social spectrum, both groups were determined to defend their territory against what they saw as encroachment by hospital 'administrators' . . . it would be a few more years before we were called 'managers', courtesy of a raft of changes introduced by the government of Margaret Thatcher.

Harry Child lost his place in the pecking order with the 1982 reorganisation of NHS management. Most of the five district administrators in Essex were pensioned off, to be replaced by the 'smart young things' from London. We all had to reapply for our jobs and, as was to be the pattern for me on future NHS reorganisations, I was fortunate enough to secure a new enhanced role, and promotion.

So, in 1982, whilst maintaining two of the components of my previous role – I was no longer minute secretary – I acquired possibly the longest job title in

NHS management, when I became 'Administrator, Planning, Commissioning and Collaboration with Local Authorities' for the newly created Mid Essex Health Authority.

The most enjoyable part of my new role was working closely with the four local hospital administrators to help them design, build and commission,(i.e. open), their new facilities. I spent a lot of time lobbying the RHA in London, to approve the centralisation of local acute services by building new facilities at Broomfield Hospital, Chelmsford. This eventually happened some years later, after a prolonged campaign not dissimilar to the one in which I was to become involved in Cambridge.

As was all too common in the NHS at this time, most of us who worked at Health Authority or regional level were on higher salaries than our colleagues at hospital level. I asked the new district administrator if he thought I was suitable for a vacancy at the hospital sector covering Braintree and Maldon. He said that I did not have enough operational experience and was 'not the sort of person' he was looking for.

So I started searching for suitable opportunities elsewhere in the NHS.

My four years in Essex had equipped me with excellent experience in designing hospital buildings, including a special care baby unit, accident and emergency department, and several wards and outpatient departments, and the writing of business plans, both of which were to come in very handy over the next 20 years.

At the age of 28, I decided that I was too young to sulk and tread water in a role that was becoming too deskbound. My temporary stints in running hospitals in Chelmsford, when covering for sickness absence, convinced me this was what I wanted to do. So, against the wishes of my girlfriend of almost two years – we had bought a house in Colchester, close to both our respective parents – I applied for a job in the West Midlands.

I was shortlisted, and attended a 'trial by lager' at a hotel near the hospital on the eve of the interview ('trial by sherry' being reserved for the appointment of senior doctors).

The people I met were very friendly, and I felt that the job was just what I wanted. One hour after my interview I was offered the position, which I immediately accepted. I telephoned Ruth to give her the news, and she was not pleased, and said, "Thank you for ruining my life. I thought we had agreed to 'give it a go'!" I suppose I needed to prove to myself that I was capable of moving away from the area I had known all my life, and make up for being a wimp and leaving Lancaster University after only one week. On the other hand, I was probably just totally insensitive to the feelings of my partner.

CHAPTER THREE

1984-88

Working in Kiddy

In March 1984 I started a new job at Kidderminster General Hospital, a sideways move on a salary equivalent of £35,000, at 2019 levels, and became the deputy unit administrator at the combined Acute and Community Unit. I was appointed largely because of my experience in commissioning new hospital buildings, and my first major task was to do just that for a 112-bed ward block for the specialties of paediatrics, obstetrics and care of the elderly.

I had wondered what it would be like working for a boss younger than myself, and assumed that it probably wouldn't happen until I was probably around 50, washed up, and on my way down and out. My boss at Kidderminster, or 'Kiddy' as the locals affectionately called it, Paul, was six weeks younger than me, six foot six tall, and with a razor-sharp wit – no doubt honed over the years from his birth and upbringing in Liverpool.

Paul was a true character, and I soon realised that the age of your boss was irrelevant; it was personality that was the determining factor.

On Fridays, Paul ordered curry and chips, with a fried egg on top, for lunch in the hospital canteen, and he and I, plus other colleagues, would pop in the Mitre Oak pub for a few pints of lager to round the week off. The others who joined us were Dave, who had a similar job to the one I had left in Essex, and whose claim to fame was booking Paul McCartney and Wings when he was social secretary of the students' union at Sheffield University. The other members of our group were Jenny and Ingrid, who regularly pulled rabbits out of hats to get locum, i.e. short-term, medical staff to this unfashionable backwater of the NHS, and Peter, our estates manager, another nice chap, except for his dodgy taste in music: he liked progressive rock, and thought that 'Tales of Topographic Oceans' by Yes was the best music ever recorded!

We were also joined by Derek and Rob, the senior managers from the Mental Health Unit, and on special occasions by Jerry – Jeremy Hallet, the overall boss, i.e. the district administrator. Sometimes we were joined by Judith, Paul's secretary, and she would have us laughing out loud at her rollercoaster love life with Max, the plumber.

My own love life was not too successful, as Ruth became homesick for Essex, despite a genuine effort on her part to settle in Kiddy, working in nearby Wolverhampton Hospital. She returned to Essex in September 1985, and following a few short-term relationships, I met Debra, my future wife, in April 1987, during a work experience placement she was undertaking at Kidderminster Hospital.

My reward for achieving the smooth completion of the three-storey block was to be chosen to escort Norman Fowler, the then secretary of state for health, when he came to officially open B Block in October 1985. Mr Fowler was due to arrive at 2.30pm, and would then go to his Sutton Coldfield constituency, as most MPs did on Fridays. Outside the Post Graduate Medical Centre, there were several dozen protestors from the public service unions, with placards criticising Thatcher's government's policy of privatisation of NHS catering, cleaning and laundry services. Whilst inside the centre, the invited guests were taking refreshments. At 1.30pm we received a message from the Department of Health saying that the secretary of state would be delayed, as the M1 was closed and they would have to do a detour. At 3.30pm we received another message from the Department of Health saying they expected the secretary of state to be with us by 5pm.

When this news was given to the assorted dignitaries, most of them decided to leave, saying they had other engagements. When I broke this news to the protestors, they too decided to roll up their placards and head off home.

In discussion with Paul, we decided to press-gang as many consultants as we could find late on a Friday afternoon, along with some other unsuspecting members of staff, and plied them with leftover sandwiches as they filled the seats vacated by the original guests.

Norman Fowler eventually arrived at 5.30pm and, not surprisingly, after spending hours in the back of a car, his first words to me were, "Where is the loo? I am bursting for a pee."

After a brief speech, Mr Fowler then spent over two hours, as originally planned, talking with patients and staff in B Block. I was impressed with his professionalism and easy-going manner, as several of my sceptical colleagues expected him to curtail his visit due to the lateness of the hour. He eventually left Kiddy at 8.30 pm.

The six of us who comprised the senior management team at Kidderminster were all around the same age, i.e. between 30–35, and relationships between the hospitals and the district headquarters were close, both geographically and personally, in this small Health Authority. It was a huge shock, therefore, when Paul failed to get the new role of unit general manager in 1986, following the government's introduction of the Griffiths Report on NHS management

Paul masked his disappointment using his Scouse wit to hide the hurt. His talent was such that he had little trouble finding another senior role in Manchester. Jerry, who had successfully applied for the new role of district general manager, felt very bad that he couldn't persuade the other interview panel members to support him and appoint Paul. He told me that if I ever had a problem with Paul's successor, to give him a call and he would 'sort things out'. It was nice to hear his words, but thankfully I never needed to take up his offer.

Smile please!

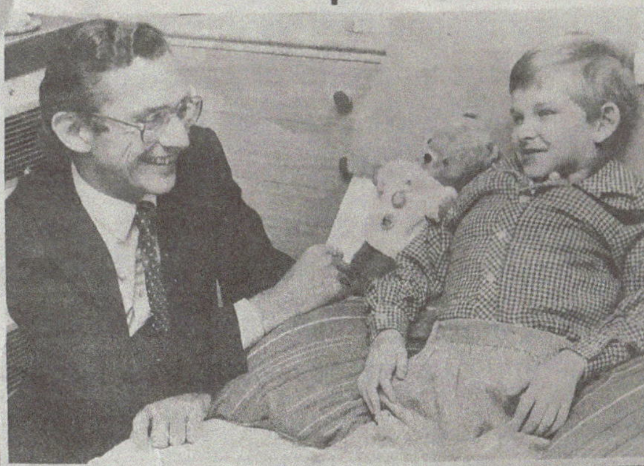

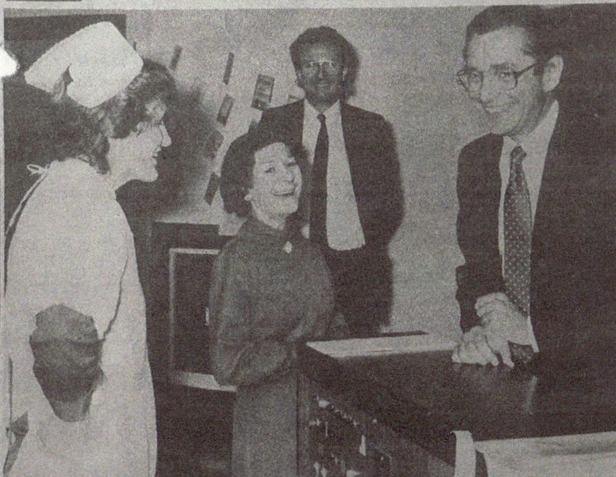

It was smiles all round when Norman Fowler arrived to open phase five at Kidderminster General Hospital.

(Above top) Mr Fowler visits nine-year-old patient Stephen [illegible]h and promises to send him a badge to add to his collection. (Above) Smiles from the hospital staff as Mr Fowler tours the wards. And (left) even smiles from Nalgo demonstrators who greeted him on his arrival.

The person appointed as unit general manager, Caroline, was the opposite of Paul, coming over as slightly aloof and cold in her personality. Once again, an NHS reorganisation had required me to reapply for my post. I did, and gained promotion, as my role had been given extra responsibilities. The most important of these was implementing new government policy that all hospital catering, cleaning and laundry/linen services had to be put out for compulsory competitive tendering, to 'test the market' against bids from private companies. A three- or sometimes five-year contract would then be awarded to the organisation who submitted the lowest priced bid.

The contract specification for the cleaning was produced by the RHA, and my task was to write the in-house bid. On several occasions the staff threatened to go on strike, and Caroline's attempts to dissuade them seemed to make matters worse. As the period for submitting tenders was drawing close, I asked Jerry to come and address the unhappy cleaning staff, who were very reluctant to accept the new patterns of working I had devised to make the in-house bid more competitive. I knew that Caroline was on leave, so Jerry, a handsome chap, put on his beige summer suit, complete with a red silk handkerchief in his breast pocket, and looked every inch the dapper English gentleman. He soon had the female workforce in his thrall as he delivered his request for the staff to 'get behind Steve Bridge' and accept the new terms and conditions and win this three-year contract. My ruse worked, the staff accepted the changes I had suggested, and they duly won the cleaning contract, beating off two external bids and delivering annual savings of £35,000 to the Health Authority.

My success in these two projects persuaded Jerry to request that Caroline give me further responsibilities and promotion.

The consultant staff at Kidderminster General Hospital were a powerful group, but I endeared myself to the anaesthetists by some hard negotiations with a medical equipment company, whose ventilators and other kit used in Intensive Care failed to meet the performance standards quoted. Drawing on my previous experience in hard bargaining, I managed to get the equipment replaced and obtain a £40,000 rebate for the hospital's League of Friends, the hard-working band of volunteers who had generously purchased these items.

For a depressed area with high unemployment, the citizens of the Wyre Forest district were very generous towards their local hospital, one of the smallest district general hospitals in the NHS. The League of Friends met monthly, often chaired by the formidable Lady Eddy. I attended these meetings, accompanied by the chairman of the Medical Advisory Committee, Dr Richard Taylor, who served as an independent MP for Wyre Forest between 2001–2010.

As the meetings took place at 7pm, and often went on for several hours, Richard and I would take it in turns to have our pagers activated by the hospital switchboard,

ERMINSTER SHUTTLE Delivered Free to 27,284 homes weekly VFD
T NEWS Delivered Free to 7,900 homes weekly VFD
ERMINSTER TIMES Average weekly sales 3,519 (July — Dec 1986)
THURSDAY OCTOBER 29, 1987

es ob b

ming from last year's ncert, also featuring bert Plant and other tists and this led the yre Forest Council to ll the curtain down on s year's show.

But promoter John mbe said they hoped make the concert an ual event and would to bring it back to urport next year.

Exception

I would have thought council could have de an exception once ear for a show that being held for char-" said Mr Combe. "It bit disappointing."

yre Forest District cil Chief Executive, Alan Dick, said he erstood the event not a rock concert a 'heavy metal' t.

Dick revealed the cil received a com- e complaint, follow- last year's event, around 30 local resi- s.

said: "The Civic is so close to re- tial property we we just can't allow concert."

Hospital returns life-saving monitors . . .

Firm pays back cash

Kidderminster health chiefs have been forced to return more than £40,000 worth of life-monitoring equipment, slamming it as "unreliable."

The intensive care unit monitors were bought by Kidderminster General Hospital just two years after a massive fund-raising drive.

EXCLUSIVE

by SIMON CRUMP

The manufacturers, Gambro Ltd, have given the Bewdley Road hospital a complete refund and the money will be used to buy replacement equipment.

In the interim period doctors will be using old equipment, which was in operation before the machines were introduced, to monitor patients who have sustained multiple injuries or suffered heart attacks.

Kidderminster Hospital's League of Friends conducted the campaign to buy the monitors, raising £28,000 themselves, with a £10,000 contribution from the British Heart Foundation and £3,000 from the Women's Royal Voluntary Service.

Mr Steve Bridges, director of operational services at KGH, said they had not "gone back to the dark ages" and patients' health was not endangered even though they had temporarily lost the facility for automatic 'early warning' which the monitors provided.

He said: "The monitors didn't perform as we felt they should and therefore we took steps to get our money back. They didn't do the job they were expected to do and they were unreliable."

League of Friends chairman, Mr David Wase, said their efforts were not wasted as the money they raised would still be used to buy replacement equipment.

He said: "We were aware there were problems to the extent the hospital would have to possibly consider replacing the equipment."

Mr Robert Smith, Divisional Officer for Gambro Ltd in Sidcup, Kent, said they knew from other installations all over the country there was nothing wrong with the equipment.

Problems

He said the problems in Kidderminster had been caused by lack of communication brought about when the original manufacturers, Kone, were taken over by Gambro Ltd.

"There was no reason to withdraw the equipment, morally, ethically or from a business point of view," said Mr Smith.

"We did it purely as a public relations exercise to stop any 'mud slinging'."

thereby giving us a reason to slip out of the meetings at around 9pm – an old trick widely practised by NHS administrators when they got bored in meetings!

Jerry was also keen that I regularly visited a tiny hospital near the Welsh border in a town called Tenbury Wells. Famous for its mistletoe market, it was also home to several wealthy people who retired there from the Birmingham area. The hospital only had 12 beds, with a small treatment room/operating theatre. If the locals suspected that the 'bosses' in Kidderminster were thinking of closing it, they quickly raised £50,000 to pay for a modest extension or a new piece of medical equipment.

During my monthly visits to Tenbury Wells, the matron made sure I was given a huge lunch of roast beef and all the trimmings. There was clearly another motive behind Jerry's request, as he confided one night in the pub that he had a vasectomy performed there, being more discreet than Kidderminster Hospital. He was proud of the Health Authority's reputation for efficiency, and cited the multitasking of the hospital handyman at Tenbury who, having collected the rubbish and put it in the incinerator, then popped up in theatre, where he scrubbed up and gave Jerry a pre-op shave/Brazilian!

My final major project was managing the conversion of a 22-bed hospital in nearby Stourport-on-Severn into one of the first units in the country for patients suffering from Alzheimer's disease. Having underspent on the £33,000 allocated by the RHA for furniture and equipment, I ingratiated myself with the clinical staff in D Block (psychiatric) in Kidderminster Hospital by spending the remaining £3,000 on new beds for their wards, and hoped that the RHA wouldn't find out.

D Block had been a nice little earner for me in my early days in Kiddy, as when I was on call I would often be required to go in around midnight and witness a patient being sectioned, i.e. detained under the terms of the Mental Health Act. I think we could claim £5 per occasion, and during some weeks on call this might happen up to a dozen times. Modifications in the process meant that most people were later 'sectioned' during normal working hours, curtailing this nice little income stream!

Meanwhile, back in Stourport, the official opening of the newly refurbished Lucy Baldwin Unit, named after the wife of the former prime minister, Stanley Baldwin (a local family), was due to be performed by the famous playwright and all-round genius, Dr Jonathan Miller, who was president of the Alzheimer's Society. Having personally made sure that we planned everything in fine detail, including a nice commemorative plaque, we were expecting a lot of local VIPs to come, and get good press coverage for this pioneering unit.

I was therefore none too pleased when two days before the opening ceremony, we were informed that Dr Miller would not now be coming as he had accepted an offer to produce an opera in Italy.

The local mayor was more than happy to step in as a last-minute replacement.

After deputising for Caroline on several occasions over an 18-month period, I decided to try and reach the top rank of NHS hospital management and become a unit general manager in an acute hospital. The Griffiths Report, commissioned a few years earlier by Margaret Thatcher, had led to an overhaul of the NHS management system. This reorganisation, only four years after the previous one, replaced the flat structure where administrators, nurses, doctors, accountants and estates staff were equal, reporting 'up the line' to their tribal bosses, and hence making decision-making slow. Griffiths put in a hierarchical system, with a general manager in charge. It was hoped that a new breed of dynamic managers would fill these new roles, at regional, district and unit (local) level. In particular, the government hoped to attract an influx of new blood from the private sector and the armed services. However, the results were very different, with the vast majority of the general manager roles going to existing NHS administrative staff. Doctors, i.e. those at consultant level, who participated in management on a part-time basis carried on much the same way as before, given that their contracts were held at the RHA. Their status was akin to that of barristers, and it was said they worked *at* hospitals, not *for* hospitals – these institutions being regarded as their 'chambers' rather than their core place of employment.

The position of unit general manager at Papworth Hospital was advertised early in 1988, and I was invited for interview in March. The units of acute hospitals, mental health and community services, were graded according to their budgets, level one being the highest – usually the large teaching hospitals – with level five the smallest, usually community services. Papworth was level four.

Papworth Hospital, based in the village of Papworth Everard, ten miles west of Cambridge, was a small specialist centre which, with two other small units – Hinchingbrooke Hospital, and the community unit – comprised the Huntingdon Health Authority. The special feature of this body was that John Major was the local member of Parliament, and he had played a crucial role in getting this very small Health Authority established in 1982. This was followed by the decision to build the smallest district general hospital in England, at Huntingdon.

At no time during my pre-interview visits was the future of Papworth Hospital mentioned, so it was in blissful ignorance that I attended the interview. The panel were mainly interested in the ability to deal with media pressure, given that the leading-edge work of Papworth was still controversial in some quarters, i.e. the ethical issues around the process of heart and lung transplantation. I sought to convince the panel of my experience in managing the media, citing my hosting of potentially controversial visits to Kidderminster of Norman Fowler in 1986, and David Steel, leader of the Liberal Democrats on his Battle Bus during the 1987 General Election campaign.

I felt the interview went well, and was delighted to be offered the job. I was sad to leave Kiddy, and had spent four very happy years there, but the 'old team' had moved on to pastures new, and I was about to enter a new chapter, both professionally and personally, as Debra and I decided to get married in October 1988.

CHAPTER FOUR

1988

Nobody Mentioned that at the Interview!

My start date was to be 6th June. During the intervening period, three 'royal' visits to Papworth were arranged: first the Duchess of Kent, to open a new cardiac catheterisation suite, then a secret visit from Margaret Thatcher and, finally, on my second day in my new job, Princess Diana. Her Royal Highness attended in her capacity as Patron of the British Lung Foundation, and came to celebrate the success of the lung transplant programme. After leaving Papworth, Princess Diana went to Newmarket Hospital, where she officially opened the Assisted Ventilation Unit. These high-profile visits made me realise how this small specialist hospital on the edge of the Cambridgeshire fens consistently punched above its weight.

No sooner had the dust settled on these important visits than I was made fully aware of the debate about the future of Papworth Hospital. My boss at Huntingdon,

HRH Princess Diana visiting Papworth Hospital in June 1988

District General Manager Keith Heron, made it very clear that should the RHA decide that Papworth become part of Addenbrooke's, then not only would this signal the end of Papworth but it would also lead to the demise of Huntingdon Health Authority.

Unbeknown to Keith or me at that time, Huntingdon's days were numbered anyway, as John Major had been a leading member of the government working party, drawing up plans for sweeping NHS reforms, including devolving power from health authorities to hospitals.

I soon became aware of the historical tensions within Papworth, and the rivalry with Addenbrookes resulting from issues arising from the development of heart and lung transplantation, also the natural rivalry between leading-edge hospitals respectively.

Within Papworth some of the tensions were exacerbated by the different funding streams. Transplantation got its money direct from the Department of Health; cardiology and cardiac surgery, classified as 'regional specialties' were overseen by the RHA; whilst respiratory medicine and thoracic surgery, defined as 'district services', were overseen by the Huntingdon Health Authority.

Just as I joined Papworth, the first consultant cardiologist appointed in 1959, Dr Hugh Fleming, was coming up to retirement. Hugh was very kind towards me and told me of the major trials and tribulations Papworth had experienced over the past 30 years.

When he set up the cardiac unit at Papworth, the reaction he got from some of the senior medical staff at

Papworth to close in 1980s

Herts Post 6. 12. 79

Papworth Hospital, where two successful heart transplant operations have been carried out this year, will be closed in the ,0s and replaced by a new unit, possibly ι Addenbrooke's Hospital, Cambridge.

The 135-bed hospital, built in 1918 for tuberculosis patients, is regarded as outmoded and too isolated. Discussions are going on to find a replacement site in the Cambridge health district and Addenbrooke's has been mentioned as a possibility.

by Rosemarie Whittaker

The administrator of the regional health authority, Mr Sidney Smith, said this week: 'The accommodation was never designed for what it is now being used for. It is in some ways old and outmoded and in isolation, whereas it should be in association with other services. It ought really to be in a general hospital.'

Mr Smith said that a decision would be made some time next year about a new site.

As well as its well-known successes with heart transplants there have been hundreds of major operations on hearts and lungs at Papworth. In the six years ending December 1978, 1,208 open-heart operations were performed on patients whose ages ranged from two to 78. The overall success rate was 94.7 per cent.

Patients are referred to Papworth from all over East Anglia and usually stay for up to three weeks to recover from surgery.

A proposed timetable for the closure appears in the strategic plan for health services in the east, published yesterday. It says that the move to a new site may start in 1985 and finish in 1987.

But Mr Smith said that these were not firm proposals and consultations were still taking place.

LESS MEETINGS

The need for pruning administration is emphasised in the ten-year plan for health services in East Anglia published yesterday.

Lines of demarcation should be sorted out to cut out the present duplication of effort, it says.

'Steps must also be taken to simplify the pattern of organisation so that less effort is

also points out a need for improved training in industrial relations to avoid the sort of disputes which are now upsetting the health service.

All staff should receive training on the rights, duties and responsibilities connected with their employment.

'The greatest contribution that could emerge from such training, would be in the reduction of industrial disruption and improved co-operation between staff and management in running the service.'

A plea for more money has gone with the new plan to the Secretary of State. Sir Arthur South, chairman of the East Anglian Regional Health Authority, has pointed out that this is a financially - deprived region with a rapidly growing population.

The greatest problem will be in paying for facilities for the over 75s. The number of East Anglians in this age group is expected to rise by 34 per cent in ten years, compared with 25 per cent nationally.

● Mr Keith Castle, the 52-year-old retired builder from London who received a new heart in August, is now Britain's longest surviving transplant patient.

On Monday it was 108 days since the transplant was carried out. The longest patient to survive had died after 107 days ten years ago.

Two weeks ago surgeons at

Addenbrooke's was dismissive: "We have no need of a cardiologist, but we suppose you will find something to do." Dr Fleming had the foresight to set up clinics in the major towns of East Anglia, which helped establish the 'hub-and-spoke' system, still one of the pillars of success for Papworth Hospital over 50 years later.

After eight years working single-handed, a second consultant cardiologist was appointed: Dr David Evans. The relationship between the two was acrimonious from the start, and in Hugh Fleming's words: "Thus began twenty years of hell."

Terence English had fought a long and hard battle to get permission to start heart transplantation at Papworth Hospital, and much of the struggle he encountered is set out in his book *Follow Your Star*.

After starting as a consultant cardiothoracic surgeon at Papworth and Addenbrooke's in 1972, Terence obtained two weeks' study leave the following year to visit Stanford University and the Mayo Clinic in the USA. He left Stanford impressed by what had been achieved during the preceding five years, and feeling that England should have at least one centre where transplantation of the heart was being pursued. A positive meeting was held in October 1973 with Roy Calne, the professor of surgery at Addenbrooke's, who had made significant achievements in kidney and liver transplantation. Also present were the two Papworth cardiologists, Hugh Fleming and David Wainwright-Evans. In Terence's words: "Hugh Fleming was neutral in his stance; whereas David Evans expressed strong opposition on both clinical and religious grounds and, subsequently, during all the years that followed, remained highly critical of the work, even to the extent of publicly accusing me of removing donor hearts from people who were still alive."

Because of the existence of Roy Calne's transplant programme, and the related availability of donor organs, it was envisaged that the heart transplant would take place under the auspices of the Department of Surgery at Addenbrooke's. As a preliminary, it was agreed that some routine cardiac surgical operations should be undertaken at Addenbrooke's, and this happened in the autumn of 1974, with Terence English and Roy Calne operating together.

Then, in Terence's words: "However, in March 1976 this arrangement ended. On my return from a meeting in Hong Kong, I was amazed to learn that during my absence Roy Calne had decided to proceed with a transplant if a donor heart could be found. In the event, this was not possible, and the patient died just one week after I had seen him. However, the reaction to Roy's decision at Addenbrooke's was intense, and we were forcefully reminded of our agreement to seek approval from the medical committee before embarking upon clinical cardiac transplantation at Addenbrooke's. And so it was that I began to believe that the best place for the programme to be developed was at Papworth Hospital."

In 1977, Michael Petch was appointed as third consultant cardiologist at Papworth and Addenbrooke's, and he agreed to provide cardiological support to the transplant programme.

Terence English presented his protocols for a heart transplant programme at Papworth to the transplant advisory panel of the Department of Health in November 1978, and was received sympathetically; but a few weeks later the chief medical officer wrote to him saying that there was no money for a programme and the department did not want to see any 'one-off' transplants. Terence English was determined to go ahead, and managed to persuade the chair of the Area Health Authority, Pauline Burnett, to approve funding for two transplants, after which he would have to find funding from elsewhere. Hence the ground-breaking heart transplant programme started at Papworth, and the rest, as they say, is history!

In August 1979, a second transplant was carried out at Papworth on the patient Keith Castle and, in Terence's words: "He subsequently became the best possible advertisement for cardiac transplantation." By the time Keith Castle left Papworth, he had already become somewhat of a national figure, and remained so for the five-and-a-half years of his subsequent life. Later in 1979, due to the wise and persistent diplomacy of Sir John Butterfield (Regius Professor of Physic), an agreement was reached as to how Roy Calne and I might collaborate in the future. Roy Calne assisted in the third heart transplant carried out at Papworth in November 1979.

In February 1980, the Cambridge Area Health Authority – Papworth's managing organisation until their abolition in 1982 – made recommendations to the RHA and the Department of Health and Social Services that "a programme of heart transplant work be undertaken at Papworth Hospital on the understanding that the cost is not charged to the normal revenue funding of the AHA."

The following month, on 13th March 1980, Patrick Jenkin, the current secretary of state for health and social services, announced in Parliament that he had "accepted Papworth Hospital as suitable for a planned programme of heart transplantation." The secretary of state pledged £100,000 of capital monies to upgrade the operating theatres and intensive care, in the knowledge that Terence English had secured a charitable donation of £300,000 from the Cambridge philanthropist, David Robinson. (£1.7million in today's money.)

The transplant surgical team was strengthened by the appointment of John Wallwork in 1981, who, Terence noted, "had gained valuable experience in the use of cyclosporine and with heart-lung transplantation during his time a chief resident at Stanford (California)."

However, while we were gaining valuable additions to our surgical staff, we lost our local cardiological support, as Michael Petch withdrew from further involvement in the heart transplant programme at the beginning of September 1980. This was a bitter blow, which I felt was partly a result of the never-ending pressure he had been subjected to by his colleague, David Wainwright-Evans. As Terence states in his book: "And so we continued . . . with Papworth surgeons and radiologists taking on the cardiac biopsies, right-heart catheters and angiograms previously done by cardiologists."

The Department of Health and Social Services provided funding to the Papworth and Harefield heart transplant programmes under the newly established Supra Regional Services Scheme, which went to highly specialised clinical services covering a population substantially larger than any one health region.

In 1988, Papworth employed 23 consultant medical staff, many of whom also worked at Addenbrooke's. They wielded great power, but also provided a fantastic service to their patients. Together with the nursing and other clinical staff, they were instrumental in helping to create the outstanding environment, or ethos, essential to the successful recovery of the patients. The consultants were publicly united in their support for Papworth to be absorbed into Addenbrooke's; however, in private several of them expressed to me their hope that Papworth could be redeveloped on its existing site, and not move to Cambridge.

The message I received from my district general manager was reiterated by the real boss some days later. Air Vice Marshall Reggie Bullen, chairman of Huntingdon Health Authority, made it abundantly clear to me that my job was to say why Papworth must stay at Papworth. Reggie was a delightful person, who after a distinguished career in the Royal Air Force, including outstanding bravery in World War II, became the next-door neighbour to John Major when, in 1977, he was

12 CAMBRIDGE EVENING NEWS, Thursday, August 25, 1988

Letters

Papworth is here to stay

I SHOULD be grateful to address some of the points raised by your front page report "Heart unit is hit by crisis" (August 12).

First of all I feel that the use of the word exodus was misleading as only seven nurses out of a total of 40 on the Intensive Care Unit have left since January 1 this year. However, coming at a time when we plan to open the Progressive Care Area this has obviously not helped at all, and the new staff have instead had to be deployed on the ICU.

Secondly, we are quite sure that the reasons why nurses leave Papworth has absolutely nothing to do with "doubts about the hospital's future"; we shall be here for many years to come.

For at least 10 years

Rather, the reasons tend to be career-linked ie either the nurse or her husband has obtained promotion involving a move out of the area or they have been successful in obtaining a place on a further training course, which in turn benefits the NHS as a whole.

Similarly, there is no foundation for stating that nurses have been leaving because of "the heavy workload and high technology associated with open heart surgery."

I would also like to reassure your readers that training for nurses does not lead to "gaps on the wards" because the work is undertaken by student nurses, but always under the supervision of a trained member of the nursing staff.

Finally if I may turn to the future of Papworth Hospital, all of us here strongly believe that it is in the best interests of the patient for us to stay in our present location. The outcome of the present Option Appraisal exercise is not yet known but we shall be here for at least the next decade and we aim to continue providing top quality care with our skilled, friendly and tremendously loyal staff.

S J BRIDGE
Unit General Manager.
Papworth Hospital,
Papworth Everard.

chosen as Conservative parliamentary candidate for the Huntingdonshire constituency. Reggie Bullen was also very well connected via his role as Bursar of Gonville and Cauis College at the University of Cambridge.

Following the appointment of a new regional general manager, Alasdair Liddell, in the summer of 1988, the previously deferred 'option appraisal' exercise into the configuration of acute hospital services in the southwest quadrant of the East Anglian Region was relaunched. Ostensibly looking at the future of hospitals at Ely and Newmarket, the real 'elephant in the room' was the future of Papworth Hospital. Since 1952, the question had been asked: should this highly regarded hospital be redeveloped in its present location, or be absorbed into the impersonal, but excellent Addenbrooke's Hospital, on its congested site in Cambridge?

Regardless of the outcome, I was determined to send out a confident and defiant message, that whatever the result, Papworth would be staying in its present location for at least ten years, so let us get on with the job of providing high quality care for the thousands of potential patients who looked to this great institution for their treatment.

CHAPTER FIVE

1989-1990

Growing the Business

Early 1989 began with Mrs Thatcher launching her government's White Paper on the NHS called 'Working for Patients'. This set out proposals for the most radical reforms of the NHS since its inception in 1948. One of the most contentious ideas was to grant self-governing status to the best performing hospitals, which would lead them to directly employ the consultant medical staff. I saw these reforms as a great opportunity for Papworth staff to come together, and as a united group have a much bigger say in the future of our hospital.

My strategy had two main themes: first, to expand, so as to achieve critical mass; and, second, to develop a strong and united team. As things stood in late 1989, there was a real risk that the hospital would be split into at least two parts, with respiratory medicine going to Hinchingbrooke Hospital and everything else being absorbed into Addenbrooke's.

There was a small management team at Papworth, including Ellen Kemp as director of nursing, and Zillah Heffer, whose role was similar to that which, in later years, became the director of operations. Ellen and Zillah were very loyal, and helped me enormously when the hospital expanded quite quickly. A couple of years later they were assisted by Sue Jervis, a middle-grade nursing officer whom I had persuaded to become one of the six operational managers (for cardiac, thoracic, transplant, pathology, radiology, and operating theatres/critical care). This structure served the hospital well, and was not felt necessary to change it for 25 years.

I was also able to persuade, sometimes cajole, members of the consultant medical staff to take on the role of clinical directors of the six management divisions. Together with the four other corporate roles leading research, education, clinical audit and the medical director role, this meant that in the early 1990s, Papworth had one-third of its senior medical staff actively involved in the running of their hospital – the highest proportion, I suspect, of any hospital in the NHS.

By the time I retired, just over 20 years later, the number of consultants had increased to 70, and the proportion involved in management was still near the one-third mark, as the massive explosion in patient numbers meant that each of the six divisions appointed their own leads for research, education and clinical governance.

A lot of NHS managers try to win the respect of senior clinical colleagues by writing 'strategic visions' for their hospital/trust. In my experience, you are more likely to win them over by more practical means. In the summer of 1989, the famous Papworth duck pond was drying up due to severe cracks in its clay base, and I wasted no time in finding a specialist company capable of carrying out the extensive work, obtaining Reggie Bullen's approval to use the charitable funds to meet the £25,000 cost of the work. Ultimately, two-thirds of the bill was paid out of the proceeds of a successful fundraising campaign, which caught the imagination of the public and former patients.

Thus, my early reputation was secured: Steve Bridge saved the duck pond!

My good relations with the chairman, Reggie Bullen, came in handy a couple of months later when, during a short break in Norfolk, I awoke to hear Papworth heading the 7am news on the Today radio programme, with "top heart surgeon says patients' lives are at risk due to shortage of intensive care nurses. Mr Francis Wells, of Papworth Hospital . . ."

In those days, hospital consultants/senior doctors, often went public and aired their concerns, without informing the hospital authorities beforehand. This was largely because their contracts were held by the RHA, and they could also appeal against dismissal direct to the secretary of state for health. (This would change with the sweeping NHS reforms of the Thatcher government, which would come into place in April 1991.)

I thought my brief holiday was over, but a reassuring telephone call with Reggie Bullen, during which I explained all the actions were underway to solve the problems raised by Mr Wells, so that we could open the recently expanded intensive care unit (now 12 beds), ended with him telling me to stay the extra two days, as planned, and he would field any hostile media enquiries, or telephone calls from the RHA or the Department of Health.

Two other things that enhanced my reputation with the senior clinical staff in 1989 were the construction and opening of a 12-bed extension to the surgical block, and negotiating a successful outcome to a dispute with a multinational drug company.

The 12-bed extension had been halted, just before I started, due to the person in charge of estates, based in the Health Authority headquarters in Huntingdon, insisting upon a ludicrously large fire escape, about one-third of the total size of the building, which sent the scheme way over budget. I circumvented this person, and enlisted the support of a senior person in the regional estates department, based in Cambridge. I had formed a good working relationship with this person, John Yates, during my dealings with him on the future of Papworth, and together we were able to come up with a much more appropriately sized fire escape, which met NHS standards, and put the scheme back within budget. My philosophy of 'don't get mad, get even' had worked well, and the new extension opened early in 1990.

The district estates manager kept his distance from me from then on, but used to give the hospital estates manager, Colin, a gentle soul, a lot of grief, which today would be classified as bullying. Interference from out-of-touch officials in district headquarters came to an end in April 1991, with the introduction of the purchaser/provider separation, and the internal market, which at last let me get on with the job I had been hired to do.

The other episode that endeared me to some of the consultant medical staff was my handling of a tricky, ethical and potentially financially disastrous issue with a leading drug company. The company wanted to end its free supply of a very high-cost drug to Papworth, which kept patients with pulmonary hypertension alive until they were able to have a heart lung transplant (or sadly died before a transplant was possible, due to the huge shortage of donor organs). Other cheaper drugs were now being used, but four patients remained on this very high-cost drug, which would cost £500,000 per annum per patient, i.e. £2 million a year – 20% of the total hospital budget.

A meeting was convened, which I chaired, and after four hours of intense discussions the four representatives of the company agreed to the compromise put forward by the lead Papworth consultant, Tim Higenbottam and myself. This was to defer the introduction of charges for six months, to see if the recent increase in the number of intensive care beds, from seven to 12, would enable Papworth to carry out more transplants, hopefully including the four patients on this drug, and hence resolve the problem.

Within six months, two of the four patients did get their transplant, but sadly the other two patients died before they got the chance.

The main issue of 1990 was the continuing struggle to persuade the region to honour their previous commitments for capital investment at Papworth. Two schemes had previously been agreed, with a big chunk of the money to come from the Department of Health body responsible for funding the transplant programme. This group, called the Supra Regional Services Advisory Group, had given its backing to an extension housing two operating theatres, and a dedicated outpatients department for transplant patients. However, it was the RHA who ultimately called the shots, i.e. as to whether these projects should proceed.

The tender prices for the operating theatres submitted by the various bidders all came in about 15% or £250K over the budgeted allocation, and no one at regional level was prepared to argue for additional money for Papworth, given its uncertain future. The problem was compounded by the fact that although the tenders for the much less expensive outpatient department scheme came in on budget, this could not physically proceed until the building containing the operating theatres was open, due to complex engineering issues on this old site.

I was determined to get the operating theatre extension built, knowing that this much-needed facility would double our surgical capacity, and hence was critical for our strategy of expansion. Conversely, the abandonment of this project could hasten the demise of Papworth, and make it easier to carve us up and transfer our services to several hospitals around the region.

I set about looking in the construction industry magazines in the hope that I would find some other companies who could deliver the project within the budget of £2.2 million. After several weeks of fruitless searching, I came across a company, based in Scotland, who claimed to provide 'system solutions' at much lower prices.

I arranged to meet with two representatives from this company for lunch in London, where they were attending an industry seminar. I hoped to convey a sense of calm authority, so naturally omitted to mention the difficulties we had experienced in getting approval for this scheme. I must have been engrossed in my presentation, and paid little attention to placing my order for lunch. When my plate of raw mince, topped off by a raw egg – steak tartare – arrived, I realised I had misread the menu. I tried to disguise my unease, and consumed my meal as if it was something I ate every week. On the train journey back to Cambridgeshire, I thought to myself, *Blimey, the things I do for Papworth . . .*

This company had recently built some theatres at a private hospital in Taunton, so I asked Terence English, recently elected as president of the Royal College of Surgeons, if he could have a look at them when he was next in the West Country on his college duties. Terence kindly viewed the theatres in February 1990 and, to my great relief, gave them his stamp of approval. My next task was to persuade the RHA to reopen the procurement exercise and, if necessary, go for a single tender to this company. The NHS, in my 14 years of experience to date, rarely used that course of action, but I pestered the regional finance director and the regional estates manager to give it a go. They promised to get back to me, as they needed to win over their regional executive colleagues, and who, I had heard on the grapevine, strongly disapproved of sanctioning major sums of capital investment at Papworth.

Whilst the above was taking place, the RHA agreed that Huntingdon Health Authority should manage the process for the Papworth section of the option appraisal exercise.

Meanwhile, the politics were getting hot, first with our constituency MP Sir Anthony Grant urging me to organise a 'Save Papworth' campaign, and then with two Papworth consultants breaking rank with their colleagues by going to see John Major, in May 1990, to express their views that Papworth should be redeveloped on its existing site. One of the consultants who met Mr Major was Michael Petch, who, as chair of the Papworth Medical Advisory Committee, was now about to perform a U-turn and propose that Papworth should not move to Cambridge.

Eighteen months earlier, Dr Petch had written to the regional medical director, Mike O'Brien, strongly supporting a move to Cambridge. His letter ended as follows:

"The above are the medical arguments for merging Papworth with Addenbrooke's. All medical men, and my two committees in particular, give strong support to these arguments. We appreciate there may be other and perhaps in the end more important considerations, but the medical arguments must be made clear to the members of the Authority. Our present fear is that they may have been 'filtered' before they reach you."

As news leaked of their meeting with John Major, the consultant in charge of one of Papworth's three medical management divisions, Tim Higenbottam, the clinical lead for thoracic services, and one of the leading 'pro-Cambridge' consultants, wrote to the RHA chairman, Colin Walker, to say:

"We were surprised to learn of the possible misrepresentation of our views by Dr Petch. We wish to set the record straight in that we, (the Thoracic Division), along with a majority of the Papworth Consultant staff at the Papworth Medical Advisory Committee when the matter was last discussed in detail (November 1989), felt that the best location for Papworth was within the Addenbrooke's campus."

I was not copied in to this letter, nor was the Huntingdon Health Authority. Dr Higenbottam soon received a stern rebuke from Reggie Bullen, stating that as the region had asked Huntingdon to manage the process for the future of Papworth Hospital, then he should have been copied in on such an important letter. Further, Reggie sought, and received, an assurance from Tim to support the efforts I was making to get the money to upgrade and expand the facilities so desperately needed at Papworth.

Another idea I was keen to take forward in order to cement my strategy of 'growing the business' was to try and build a private patient ward, given the strength of this market for cardiac services. I wrote a business plan, which I got the major finance firm – Peat Marwick McClintock, it was called in those days – to polish, and the interest from the big private medical companies was very strong. However, as I could not promise more than a seven-year tenure on the existing site, we were unable to reach a deal.

I then turned to the Reggie Bullen for support, and he jumped at the idea, since he felt that the more capital investment we could obtain, then the greater the chance of Papworth being redeveloped on its existing site. Reggie agreed to my suggestion that I could borrow half a million pounds from Papworth's charitable funds, which would be paid back from the profits which the 22-bed private ward would generate. Relieved to get this decision, I then had to try my luck with the region to secure the remaining half a million pounds of capital I needed.

Bearing in mind they had not yet agreed to reopen the operating theatre procurement process, it was with some trepidation that I submitted my business plan to Paul Kemp, regional finance director. I rather took the view, 'in for a penny, in for a pound', as I asked the region to inject even more of their money into Papworth at this highly sensitive time. They played for time by allowing us to proceed with the small scheme for the transplant outpatient department, which, in view of the hospital's uncertain future, we agreed to settle for portable type building solution.

With the NHS reforms programme gathering pace, I held discussions with all of Papworth's consultant medical staff, now 25 in number, to seek their support for us to express an interest in applying for self-governing hospital status.

In October 1990, I organised a ballot of the consultants, hoping to gain their support to enable me to submit an application to become an NHS 'trust' – the revised, and more politically acceptable term for self-governing units to also include community services, ambulance services and mental health services.

With 15 of the 25 consultants supporting my proposal, I wrote to Alasdair Liddell, regional general manager, to express Papworth's interest in becoming a second-wave NHS trust, i.e. from April 1992. My counterpart at Hinchingbrooke Hospital, Peter Mankin, confided to me that he was planning the same course of action. From the time we went public with our respective bids for self-governing status our relationship with our colleagues at Huntingdon Health Authority became strained, as they realised that autonomy for both of the hospitals they managed would signal the end of their brief (seven-year) existence, and a return to a Cambridge-dominated Health Authority.

CHAPTER SIX

1991

Brave New World

Despite being a pilot site for the NHS reforms, privately, and like so many other parts of the NHS establishment that would be losing their powers, our RHA believed that the Labour Party would form the next government and maintain their promise to sweep away these far-reaching NHS changes. Given this, and the region's privately held view that Papworth should be taken over by Addenbrooke's, our application for NHS trust status was given a lukewarm reception by them. Consequently, they rejected my request for a small sum of money to progress Papworth's application to become a second-wave NHS trust, i.e. from April 1992. Their letter to me, of 14th November 1990, from their director of corporate development, Stephen Thornton, whilst accepting that money had been given to other hospitals, went on to say:

> *"Clearly, in the light of the continuing uncertainty about the future location of Papworth Hospital, it would not really be appropriate for us here at the Regional Health Authority to be seen to be making sums of money available to you to take forward your application at this stage. I recognise that we run the risk of not being even handed in our approval to Trust support."*

This was followed up, four months later in February 1991, by the Regional Health Authority's formal rejection of our second-wave application for NHS trust status. Again, the uncertainty over Papworth's future location was the reason given for their decision. During my meeting with Stephen Thornton, to discuss their letter, I said that in view of their decision, the least they could do was to give me the extra money I was seeking to build the new operating theatres. Stephen said that he would convey my request to his colleagues at the region.

It was only a few weeks later, whilst in this state of organisational limbo, that I received my first overture from the new unit general manager at Addenbrooke's, John Ashbourne. He had recently moved from being district general manager of the Cambridge Health Authority and, having seen the writing on the wall, decided that a more interesting future beckoned as chief executive officer (CEO) of a prestigious teaching hospital, rather than continuing to be the boss of a 'purchaser' Health Authority.

John's predecessor at Addenbrooke's, David Astley, a well-liked and respected hospital manager, decided to take a sideways move to be the unit general manager, and eventually CEO, at the Norfolk and Norwich Hospital. John Ashbourne was an impressive character, one of the few successful 'imports' from the private sector following the implementation of the Griffiths Reports, a few years earlier. The gist of John's offer to me was that I should give up trying to achieve trust status for Papworth, and agree to a 'federal' association with Addenbrooke's. Crucial details, such as identifying a site, obtaining planning permission, and securing funding, were missing in John's brief paper. The details, he stressed, would be thrashed out later, but for now, I 'needed to see the big picture'.

This was a phrase that was regularly said to me over the coming decade, especially when I asked for more detail or evidence to support a view that Papworth should give up its fight to determine its future.

Should I not respond favourably to his offer, John gave a strong hint that Addenbrooke's would develop their own cardiothoracic unit, a view subsequently confirmed by the University of Cambridge in their formal response to the option appraisal two months later:

> *"The prospects for Papworth, were it to remain in situ or to transfer to Hinchingbrooke, give cause for concern for the reasons stated above. There is no prospect of the faculty board being in a position to undertake academic developments*

at either site, even if this were desirable, because of the level of investment required. The faculty board have already had to make alternative arrangements for meeting the teaching needs of their students in cardiothoracic medicine and surgery – subjects that are regarded by all medical schools as core curriculum subjects. Were Papworth not to transfer to Addenbrooke's, the faculty board would feel compelled to examine ways in which their interest in important areas of cardio-thoracic medicine and surgery could be protected. It is hard to see how such protection could be achieved without the development of services on the Addenbrooke's site."

Earlier, in April 1991, Huntingdon Health Authority had issued their option appraisal report, containing the four options for the future of Papworth Hospital. This was to allow three months for interested parties and the general public to send in their views as to which option they preferred. The options and their estimated costs were:

A. Partial and total redevelopment on the existing site: £15.4 million/£36.4 million, respectively;
B. Relocation to Hinchingbrooke Hospitals: £31.4 million;
C. Relocation to Addenbrooke's Hospital: £33.9 million.

John Ashbourne stepped up his lobbying of Papworth's consultants, but without copying me in on the correspondence, or inviting me to any of the dinners or meetings he arranged for them. My good relationships with my consultants ensured that they gave me copies of all correspondence, and feedback of what was discussed at these dinners/ meetings.

Whilst a majority of the Papworth consultants still favoured a move to the Addenbrooke's site, our success over the past couple of years in building three new extensions, at a cost of almost £1 million – a 12-bed surgical ward extension, facilities for nuclear medicine/ gamma camera, and transplant outpatients – with the possibility of a further £5 million in capital developments, persuaded several of them to voice their preference for option A: a partial redevelopment at Papworth Everard.

In addition, our significant growth in patient activity and financial turnover had the effect of persuading those consultants who had wanted Papworth to be absorbed into Addenbrooke's to alter their thinking, so that the move to Cambridge should now be couched in terms of being adjacent to Addenbrooke's. This view was captured by Sir Terence English in his response to Huntingdon Health Authority's option appraisal paper in the summer of 1991. He wrote:

> *"I know from my contact with patients and with friends in East Anglia that a great head of steam is building up amongst the patients and*

population of East Anglia not to touch Papworth or remove it from its present site. I have to say, however, that the information which is being generally fed to the public is very one-sided and relies on the obvious and understandable loyalty of patients to our hospital.

However, I have to restate my view that I believe that, if one looks to the long term, the best option for our services and for the patients of East Anglia would be to relocate the Regional Cardiothoracic Unit as a geographically identifiable unit on the Addenbrooke's site. I believe that this would need to be along the lines of a 'Rosie-style[2]' development, which would preserve the ethos and integrity of Papworth as a functioning unit and would, at the same time, allow us to benefit from proximity to the many other important services and scientific activities on the Addenbrooke's site, as well as to play a more effective role in the future of the medical school.

I believe, therefore, that the time has come to reduce the options to two rather than three and to allow the Regional Health Authority to present its best plans for Papworth at Addenbrooke's so that these could be properly considered alongside the alternative of staying here."

---

[2] The recently opened maternity hospital based in a separate building

On 19th July 1991, Huntingdon Health Authority convened a special meeting to consider the outcome of the three-month public consultation on the Papworth section of the southwest quadrant option appraisal.

As was never in doubt, they unanimously agreed to support option A – the partial redevelopment of Papworth on its existing site. However, because the majority of the Papworth consultants favoured the Addenbrooke's option, the RHA subsequently decided that more detailed work was required on both these two options.

A few weeks later I was informed by the region that, as it may take up to another year to complete the additional work on the Papworth option appraisal, they had reluctantly agreed to my request for £2.7 million towards the £3.2 million I needed to proceed with the two remaining capital projects currently on hold, namely, the operating theatre extension and the new 22-bed ward.

I felt sure that part of the logic for this decision was growing political pressure, as a General Election was close, and the appalling state of waiting times for heart surgery, which, at up to three years for some patients, meant that several died before they received this lifesaving operation

This was not far short of a national disgrace.

My discomfort at making the front page of *The Daily Mirror* earlier in March 1991 now seemed to be worth it!

Meanwhile, back in April 1991, the regional general manager, Alasdair Liddell, decided that all unit general managers of aspiring NHS trusts would have to undergo

DAILY Mirror

Tuesday, March 19, 1991 **NEWSPAPER FOR THE NINETIES** Est daily sale last week: 3,775,180 (INCORPORATING THE DAILY RECORD) 25p

Uproar over Major moan on heart ops

NHS BLUNDER: Premier John Major

CLANGER No 1

EXCLUSIVE
By JILL PALMER

COMPLAINTS by John Major about slow treatment at a famous heart hospital caused Budget-eve fury last night.

Medical chiefs bluntly told the Prime Minister that lives are at risk because of cash cuts by HIS government.

Mr Major dropped a clanger by sending two letters to Papworth Hospital in his Cambridgeshire constituency, demanding to know why two patients were having to wait a year for heart by-pass surgery.

For Papworth surgeons have been ordered to cut back on heart ops to save money.

Their plea for a new 30-bed ward was rejected by the Government. The hospital, which planned 800 heart operations a year, can now carry out less than 700.

Seriously ill patients face a 12-month wait for surgery. Four in five deteriorate so badly they have to be rushed in as emergencies.

Surgeon Frank Wells said: "It is a desperate situation. Waiting lists are getting longer and longer.

"I can't see any light at the end of the tunnel without more money and more beds."

Hospital manager Stephen Bridge said: "On average I get a letter a week from MPs asking why their constituents must wait so long. Two were from Mr Major.

Changes

"In our reply, we told him we can't carry out more operations without more facilities.

"We have to balance our books by the end of this year ready for the Government's NHS changes."

The hospital refuses to name the two patients Mr Major referred to.

Labour's Shadow Health Secretary Robin Cook said: "John Major can't have it both ways.

"He can't cut the NHS and then expect better hospital treatment for his voters back home."

● Comment – Page 2

TARZAN IN 'SCRAP COUNCILS' SHOCK

CLANGER No 2

By ALASTAIR CAMPBELL

BIG-SPENDING county councils may be scrapped as part of Michael Heseltine's desperate poll tax shake-up.

Tarzan's plans were leaked last night – dramatically upstaging Chancellor Norman Lamont on the eve of his first Budget.

Astonished MPs believe the Environment Secretary also intends to:

ABOLISH local education authorities and finance schools from Whitehall.

SHAKE UP the police so they are organised and funded on a national basis.

FORCE local councils

■ Turn to Page 2

LEAKED: Heseltine

a two-day assessment, an intensive course of practical and theoretical tests designed to see if we could cut it as chief executives of the new wave of self-governing hospital trusts. I remember listening to the whole of Bob Dylan's masterpiece 'Blonde on Blonde' in my car on the journey there and, to this day, I can recall the nervousness I felt before entering the hotel on that damp and misty morning.

It was very rigorous, and I remember receiving some criticism after one session from Len Fenwick, a very experienced unit general manager from Newcastle, and outside assessor, who felt I placed too much reliance on capital planning, i.e. wanting to build too many new facilities at Papworth. I remember leaving the event, at a hotel in Peterborough, feeling drained, knowing that my career was on the line.

The course participants were asked to report to Alasdair Liddell's office the following week for feedback, and presumably hear our fate. My instinct told me that I was not the type of manager that Alasdair wanted in his patch.

Whilst waiting outside his office, the previous meeting came to an end and David Leese, the very able unit general manager of Peterborough Hospital said hello, but I could sense that he was in sombre mood. I later heard that David decided not to put his name forward to be CEO at Peterborough Hospital.

When I entered Alasdair's office, he did not rise to greet me, but instead stayed sitting at a right angle to me, with both feet perched on his desk, looking out of the window. After some perfunctory words of introduction, he said that whilst my results showed I was technically very able, he did not feel that I had sufficient strategic vision to become a successful NHS trust CEO. As he delivered his verdict, he hardly turned to face me, continuing to look out of the window. He continued by saying that as he had not had much contact with me, I should speak with Paul Kemp, his finance director, as he knew we had spent a lot of time together on the option appraisal. Alasdair also suggested that I ask a couple of the Papworth consultants to forward their views of me to him, as they would be a crucial group of colleagues over the coming years.

As I left his office, my mind went back nine years to 1982, when the new district administrator at the newly formed Mid Essex Health Authority, told me that he did not think I had what it took to be a successful hospital manager[3].

As luck would have it, Paul Kemp was in his office. I told him what Alasdair had said, and his reply, not dissimilar to the John Cleese (Monty Python) Secret Service sketch, "Can you keep a secret?", "Yes" replied the applicant. "Well, you are in then," John Cleese says.

Paul's questions to me were along the following lines: "Are your finances in balance? Do you get on well with your doctors and nurses?" I replied yes to both questions.

---

[3] In keeping with another of my beliefs, 'Don't get mad, get even', I took a sideways move to Kidderminster Hospital, and spent four very successful years there, gaining two promotions, before being appointed to Papworth.

"In that case," Paul continued, "I don't see a big problem with you becoming CEO of Papworth."

Back at Papworth, I asked two of our senior consultants, Michael Petch, as chairman of the Medical Advisory Committee, and John Wallwork, who had taken over as transplant director following Terence English becoming president of the Royal College of Surgeons, if they would be so kind as to send their views of me to Alasdair Liddell. I never asked what Michael and John wrote about me, but it must have been positive, because I heard no more from Liddell on this matter.

A corollary to this bruising and emotionally draining couple of months, was that the RHA later came in for some criticism from other parts of the NHS for their severe culling of existing unit general managers. So, in response, in December 1991, the region arranged an event for those of us who had survived the Peterborough Assessment Centre, called a 'Development Workshop', held in a nice hotel in Norwich. By complete contrast with the carnage of eight months earlier, the toughest test we had to undergo was a psychometric test, and most of the sessions were about valuing your staff and avoiding a 'hire and fire' culture of management!

CHAPTER SEVEN

1992

Snatching Victory from the Jaws of Defeat

In March 1992, the RHA decided to implement one of the less contentious recommendations of the southwest quadrant option appraisal, and that was to remove acute services from Newmarket Hospital. This meant that a new location would be required for the Assisted Ventilation Unit, a specialist respiratory centre set up by Dr John Shneerson, one of the three consultant chest physicians working at Papworth. John based this unit at Newmarket, after having failed to secure the support of his consultant chest physician colleagues to house it at Papworth.

I was told by John Yates, the regional estates manager, that the region would fund a modest capital development for a new assisted ventilation unit, but that they very much hoped that Dr Shneerson would decide to locate it at Addenbrooke's. As John Ashbourne's veiled threat to set up a rival cardiothoracic service was still fresh in my mind, and Huntingdon Health Authority had suggested that some of our respiratory medicine should transfer to Hinchingbrooke, hosting the unit would be a good first step in sub-specialising Papworth's respiratory medicine portfolio. This would differentiate it from those services provided in district general hospitals, and put it on a par with Papworth's other specialised services.

I wasted no time in engaging architects and engineers to work with John Shneerson and design his new unit. I incorporated this work into the business case I had written, and submitted it to the region.

After a few weeks, I was told that my bid was successful, mainly because at £0.7 million it was 30% cheaper than the Addenbrooke's proposal and, because I was proposing a greenfield site, the Papworth option could be open within a year.

I had to pinch myself, as this meant that I now had three capital projects in the pipeline, all of which were not without risk of overrun and exceeding the budgeted cost. I knew that I would have to take an active role in the project management of these three schemes, but relished the prospect of using my extensive pre-Papworth experience in designing and building hospital schemes to prevent that from happening. John Ashbourne graciously complimented me on my victory, but added, caustically, that he felt I had bitten off more than I could chew, and that the new unit, soon to be rebranded as the Respiratory Support and Sleep Centre, would "bankrupt Papworth within two years".

This momentous year of 1992 also saw the Papworth Staff Action Group, assisted by several patient support groups, most notably the 'zipper clubs'[4], announcing that they had secured 120,000 signatures on a petition to 'Save Papworth Hospital'. This was part of the campaign I was orchestrating, at arm's length, and brilliantly managed by my recently appointed executive assistant Sally Carpenter, to persuade the RHA to back the option for redevelopment on our existing site.

In May, following John Major's unexpected election victory, RHAs were given clear instructions by the Department of Health to speed up the pipeline of NHS trust applications. I received a request from the region to resubmit our application, which would now be considered for the third wave, i.e. April 1993.

I then became aware that the chair of the Huntingdon Community Health Council, Councillor Wendy Silby, a friend of John Major, had written to him a few weeks earlier urging him to support the redevelopment of Papworth Hospital on its existing site. His reply to her, on the 2nd June was unequivocal:

> *"I am strongly in favour of Papworth remaining on its present site and not being moved to Addenbrooke's. The RHA are well aware of my views and also that I am unlikely to change them."*

---

4 An exclusive club for those who have gone through open heart surgery, leaving them with a zipper-like scar on their chest!

As part of the application process to become an NHS trust, it was necessary to put forward at least two suitable applicants as potential chairman of the trust board. I was initially given the names of several businessmen by our MP, Sir Anthony Grant in 1991, and the region also supplied a list of names. After meeting with several of these potential applicants, accompanied by several of my senior consultant colleagues, we let the region know of our preferred candidate early in 1992.

Our preferred candidate was acceptable to Sir Colin Walker, the RHA chairman, and had such an extensive range of connections that, in June, he even arranged for the band from his former army regiment, the Grenadier Guards, to play at a garden party I had organised to celebrate the successful completion of our two biggest capital schemes – the operating theatre extension and the two-storey Varrier Jones Ward, comprising 22 beds (18 of which were single rooms with en-suite facilities), a lecture theatre and a cardiac outpatients' department.

Much credit must be given to three regional colleagues for helping me get these schemes built at a time when the region would have preferred not to have put any money into Papworth. The three in question were Paul Kemp, the finance director, his deputy Ken Newitt, and John Yates, their estates manager.

In July, Paul Kemp, who had been designated as the lead director for the option appraisal exercise, told me that he would be taking a paper to their September board meeting, recommending that of the two options on the table it had been decided to support option A, the partial redevelopment on the Papworth site, at a capital cost of £15.4 million.

Following the RHA's previous agreement to allocate me the £2.7 million, I had requested for the operating theatres and Varrier Jones Ward, plus the £0.7 million for the Respiratory Support and Sleep Centre. This meant that the actual spend on the Papworth option would now be close to £20 million, a result that I was proud to achieve in these difficult circumstances.

The conclusions and recommendations in Paul Kemp's paper on the future location of Papworth Hospital were as follows:

> *"Were we planning services from scratch, there is no doubt that specialist cardio-thoracic services would be a core component of the region's teaching hospital. The ready access to all the specialised facilities that would be available to seriously ill patients; the benefits to medical education and the training of other clinical staff; and the improved opportunities for research, particularly those projects based on a multi-specialty approach, would all readily lead to that conclusion.*
>
> *However, that is not the situation which faces us. There is a substantial investment already at Papworth, not just of bricks and mortar, but of enthusiasm and commitment from the staff, support from the local community,*

and the gratitude of former patients. The further consultation undertaken by the RHA has been valuable in ensuring that the medical arguments have been heard, and are understood by the public and their representative organisations, but it has also shown beyond any doubt their commitment to keeping the services at Papworth. Whilst professional interests attach a high priority to clinical effectiveness, the consultation has shown that the public regard other factors – environmental quality, the perception of a more 'personal' service, even the ease of car parking – as important issues. In this instance their judgment is that, taken together, they outweigh the clinical arguments.

A majority of purchasing District Health Authorities, whilst recognising that the issues are quite finely balanced, also support retaining services at Papworth. Their views, too, are extremely important, both because they speak for the interests of the residents of East Anglia and because their support is a key factor in determining whether future capital investment should be made.

The clinical issues – clinical integration of services and enhancing opportunities for teaching and research – do need to be addressed. Whilst leaving services at Papworth inevitably produces a sub-optimum solution, the general manager at Papworth and Regius Professor do share a commitment to closer working and enhancing the research programme at Papworth. There is also closer liaison between Papworth and other acute hospitals regarding joint appointments of medical staff which will improve liaison and understanding to the benefit of patient care.

Recommendations:

That the Papworth board be invited to prepare a detailed business case for a phased development of facilities and services on the existing hospital site.

The Papworth board and Clinical School continue discussions on how the opportunities for teaching and research might best be enhanced and report back with proposals to the RHA."

The RHA's board meeting took place on 22nd September 1992.

They voted to support option A, the partial redevelopment of Papworth on its existing site. Pressure from Number 10 Downing Street must have been the key factor in their decision, and set the tone for Paul Kemp's paper.

Many years later I was told by one of the region's board members present that day that, midway through the meeting, the prime minister had telephoned and reiterated his view to the regional general manager, Alasdair Liddell, that Papworth Hospital should stay in the village of Papworth Everard.

Not surprisingly, the Regius Professor of Physic, Keith Peters, registered his dissent at the decision.

I was naturally very pleased with this decision, and also that Paul Kemp had accepted many of my arguments when drafting his paper, including my desire to break free of the 'isolationist' style pursued by Huntingdon, and pursue a collaborative style of working with Addenbrooke's and the University of Cambridge. Being an unashamed pragmatist, I also cast doubts on the timeliness of the Addenbrooke's option, and how soon the NHS could purchase additional land adjacent to that site, which was designated as greenbelt land and could not be built on[5].

In October 1992, I received a telephone call one evening at home from the RHA chairman, Sir Colin Walker. He was at the Conservative Party conference in Brighton, and rang to tell me that Number 10 wanted a different person to be chairman of our new trust board. Political favours were owed to somebody in the Huntingdon area, so that was that. Sir Colin asked me if I could "keep the doctors in line" after this news became public. I replied that I would do my best, but I could tell that he felt that our preferred candidate was getting a raw deal by being rejected at this late hour.

The senior doctors at Papworth who had worked with me for months to persuade our 'chairman designate'

5 My reservations proved to be well founded, as it was not until 2002 that the adjoining land to Addenbrooke's had its greenbelt classification removed.

Celebrations as Papworth stays put

Corks pop as Papworth celebrates the decision to stay on their present site.

by Matthew Arnold

AFTER decades of debate health officials this week decided to keep Papworth Hospital on its present site.

Plans to move the unit to either Huntingdon or Cambridge have finally been thrown out and the news has been greeted with enthusiasm from most quarters. Papworth's fate was sealed this Tuesday during a meeting of East Anglian Regional Health Authority.

John Prior, chairman of the staff action group, said the decision removed a dark cloud which had hung over Papworth for years.

"The staff always believed in their cause to 'Keep Papworth at Papworth' and were greatly strengthened in their fight by the support of so many organisations and people from all walks of life throughout the UK, plus over 122,000 signing our petition," he said.

"Staff from all departments and all professions are now able to continue caring for their patients without the constant uncertainty of whether the services are going to be transferred to another site. This is coupled with the danger of fragmenting teamwork which has played, and continued to play, such an important role in the success of the hospital," added Mr Prior.

Stephen Bridge, unit general manager, said he was delighted with the decision. "It means Papworth can move forward and develop services for the population of East Anglia and the rest of the field.

"What we aim to do is speedily move forward to turn our master plan into reality," he said.

The future development plan for Papworth is estimated to cost £15million compared to a figure twice that size for the Addenbrooke's relocation option.

Mr Bridge added that public opinion must have been a main factor in the decision to keep the hospital in Papworth Everard, and said the local media and the area's MPs had all added a boost to the cause.

John Kneeshaw, consultant anaesthetist, gave his reaction from the surgeon's point of view and said he was delighted to at last to have a decision. "This means we can continue our research work and build some positive links with Addenbrooke's Hospital," he said.

Although some staff had favoured the Addenbrooke's option for training convenience, Mr Kneeshaw said that as a whole, the medical component of Papworth had accepted the decision.

to relinquish many of his other commitments were livid. It was left to Sir Terence English to convey their feelings to Sir Colin Walker, which he did in a letter dated 29th October:

> *"It will not surprise you to hear that I think that ** would have been a much more effective and dynamic chairman and been better for the hospital. I also think that it is a cause for great concern that his name, which received strong support both from management and consultant staff, should have been rejected in favour of someone who, on paper and on past experience, seems to be less qualified for the job. This seems to have been an example of political machination prevailing over good sense."*

I met our new chairman designate, Dr Audrey Stenner, for the first time in early November, and instinctively felt that our relationship would not be plain sailing.

On 18th November 1992, we held the official opening ceremony of our twin operating theatre complex, performed by HRH the Duchess of Gloucester. This was the first opportunity for Audrey to meet some of my colleagues. It did not go well, as Audrey, proud of her Yorkshire heritage, was direct to say the least, and when being introduced to some of my female management colleagues commented, "It appears that you need to be blonde to work here." This was the first of several examples of Audrey's political incorrectness, and led to some difficult periods in our working relationship, which was to last over nine years.

CHAPTER EIGHT

1993

Two at the Top

Our application for NHS trust status was approved in January 1993, and I was duly appointed chief executive in February. We held our first trust board meeting on 22nd April, when I reminded the board of the RHA's mandate to us: to prepare a business case for the partial redevelopment on our existing site, at a cost of circa £15.4 million.

That seemed to fall upon deaf ears, as I was asked by the chair and three of the non-executive directors to also obtain designs and costings for a much more extensive redevelopment. Over the next few months, my executive colleagues and I prepared a business case containing six options, which we presented to the September board meeting.

The chairman and non-executives, with the exception of Professor Sir Dillwyn Williams, the University of Cambridge representative – a position we did not need to have, but one I insisted upon to demonstrate my desire to improve our academic links – pushed for the three most expensive options, ranging in cost from £30 million to £36 million. Although it was known that RHAs were to be abolished in six months' time, I advised the board not to completely disregard the mandate they had given us. I gave two reasons for this advice: the hospital would be unable to function for long periods in the full development option, given the extent of disruption the construction would bring, and second, my experience and intuition told me to grab the money on offer, as there is always a risk in NHS reorganisations – and I had experienced three in my 16-year career to date – that the successor bodies often ignored controversial decisions made by their predecessors, and embarked upon their own course of action.

The chairman and the three non-executives took the view, however, that the prime minister's support would result in a smooth passage for the scheme. Their total lack of previous NHS experience worried me, as I knew how the NHS worked; similar to Sir Humphrey in *Yes, Prime Minister*, exercising great skill in appearing to comply with the wishes of their political masters, whilst at the same time placing subtle obstacles in the way, under the guise of seeking further information, or clarification. Little did I know at the time, but this is exactly what was to happen over the next three years.

After further discussions with my non-executive colleagues, I was able to persuade them to lower their expectations, and in October 1993 we submitted a business case to the RHA for a redevelopment of the Papworth Everard site, costing £24 million.

Following our official break from the Huntingdon Health Authority on 1st April 1993, I wasted little time in my efforts to establish a good relationship with the University of Cambridge School of Clinical Medicine. The person in charge was the Regius Professor of Physic, Professor Keith Peters, and it seemed obvious to me that if Papworth was to fulfil the resolution of the RHA's September 1992 board meeting, then this was the place to start.

It had been made clear to me by my former boss at Huntingdon, on several occasions between 1988-92, that under no circumstances should I meet with Professor Peters. Now free of this small-minded attitude, I requested a meeting at the clinical school in June 1993. Keith and I seemed to hit it off, and within half an hour we had adjourned to the bar to enjoy a pint of beer. The gist of our meeting was how Papworth could demonstrate it was serious in developing our research portfolio, and the possibility of part-funding professorial chairs in respiratory medicine, and possibly cardiac surgery, over the coming years.

I had ruffled a few feathers earlier in the year by appointing a non-doctor, Noreen Caine, as Papworth's first director of research and development. Noreen had previously been the senior research manager in our transplant programme, and had a good track record of innovation. I used some of the transplant funding to establish our research and development department, and was able to give Keith Peters some practical examples of the progress Noreen and her team had made in their first few months.

I briefed Audrey Stenner on my meeting with Keith Peters, but I could tell from her reaction that she did not want me to become too friendly with him, lest that weaken my resolve to keep Papworth at Papworth Everard.

The highlight of 1993 was the second visit of Princess Diana to officially open the Respiratory Support and Sleep Centre (RSSC), only five years after performing the same ceremony when it was called the Assisted Ventilation Unit, and based at Newmarket Hospital. In my book, this was remarkable, and proved that the consultant in charge, John Shneerson, must have had superb contacts in addition to his quiet determination to develop his service. I therefore had no hesitation in supporting John in developing the RSSC, against some opposition from his colleagues, who did not regard 'sleep studies' appropriate in a hospital like Papworth. The RSSC went from strength to strength, and today is one of the largest centres of its type in Europe.

Perhaps the most significant event of 1993 was the consultant appointment panel for a chest physician, which was to be a joint appointment with Hinchingbrooke Hospital.

Huntingdon Health Authority, first in their previous role of being the 'bosses' of Papworth Hospital, until 31st

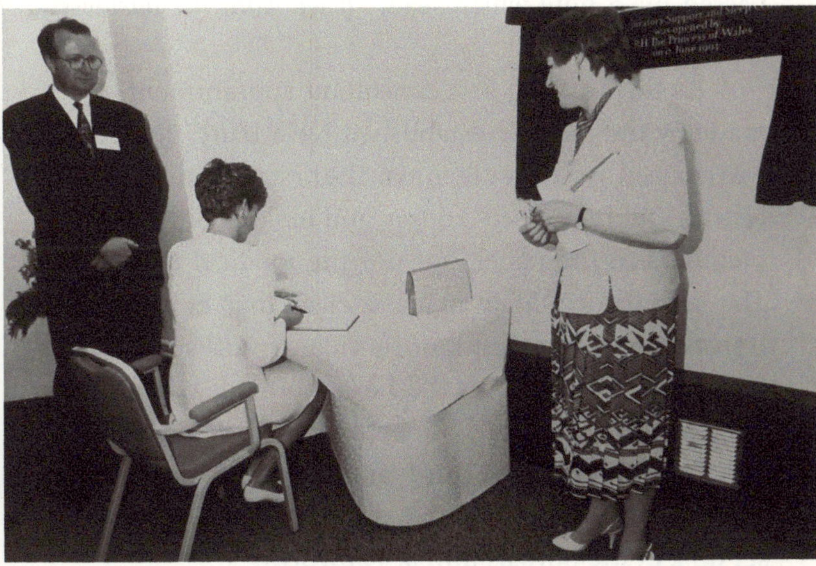

HRH Princess Diana signing the visitors' book

March 1993, and second, from 1st April 1993, our biggest 'purchaser', insisted on the joint appointment, but never fully explained the rationale for their thinking.

During the 'trial by sherry' meeting with the shortlisted candidates, the night before the interview, John Wallwork, the clinical director of the transplant programme, but not a member of the interview panel, passed me a note which read, "*If we want the business, appoint the woman.*"

As this was the first consultant appointment to be made by the recently established NHS trust, the panel was chaired by Audrey Stenner. The first candidate waxed lyrical, and impressed Audrey and me, the only two lay members of the panel, but not the medical members. The second candidate made it clear that he favoured transferring a big chunk of services from Papworth to Hinchingbrooke should he be appointed, which, not surprisingly, endeared him to the Hinchingbrooke panel members. The third and final candidate, 'the woman', was very impressive, and spoke of her desire to set up a cystic fibrosis unit at Papworth.

The panel was deadlocked, so we adjourned for lunch, during which the mystery behind the Health Authority's insistence on a joint appointment unravelled. The candidate preferred by Hinchingbrooke pulled out, and came to my office to tell me that, having had the opportunity to talk with several Papworth clinical staff, he realised that it would be clinically unviable to move services to Hinchingbrooke. He then told me what was promised at his meetings with senior Health Authority management, and my counterpart at Hinchingbrooke – a former army officer, appointed under the Griffiths initiative, and only in post at Hinchingbrooke for three months. Apparently, as part of the forthcoming annual contract negotiations, Papworth would have their money reduced by as much as £1 million to enable chest medical services to be set up in Hinchingbrooke Hospital.

I reported this to Audrey, and Frank Wells and John Shneerson, the Papworth medical representatives on the committee, and when we reconvened as a full appointments panel, the Hinchingbrooke representatives did the decent thing and there was unanimous support to appoint 'the woman'.

The woman, Diana Bilton, proved to be a great success and certainly 'brought in the business'. She went on to play a crucial role in the development of Papworth over the next 15 years, before being tempted by the bright lights of London, with an exciting opportunity to work at the Royal Brompton Hospital.

The day after the interviews, I met with the Health Authority's manager in charge of their contracting process. He apologised for the underhand manner in which they had gone about things, and said they were fearful for Hinchingbrooke's future in the new world of the 'internal market', and said that my success in beating Addenbrooke's to host the RSSC would, they believe, offset the income we would have lost.

Common sense soon prevailed, and no income was transferred from Papworth to Hinchingbrooke. Instead Papworth funded Diana Bilton's post 100%, and we agreed to pay 30% towards a new chest physician based at Hinchingbrooke, but with three sessions a week at Papworth. This arrangement attracted very good doctors from its inception in 1994, and lasted until Papworth moved to Cambridge in May 2019.

CHAPTER NINE

1994-95

Yes, Prime Minister

The new year of 1994 began with Secretary of State for Health, Virginia Bottomley, eventually agreeing to visit Papworth, on Valentine's Day, and officially open two of our capital projects: the Varrier Jones Ward, named after the founder of the hospital, and a new cardiac catheterisation suite.

She agreed to this engagement on the express undertaking that she was not to be lobbied on our redevelopment, specifically when the funding would be available. It was only a few weeks later that the new Anglia and Oxford regional office – one of eight set up to replace the former East Anglian RHA, and 13 others – informed me that all major capital projects would now have to seek funding under the new 'private finance initiative' (PFI) recently introduced by the chancellor of the exchequer, Norman Lamont.

Virginia Bottomley, Secretary of State for Health

This news effectively made the business case we had submitted to the RHA seven months earlier redundant.

As I feared, this latest NHS reorganisation meant that a new business case would have to be produced. We also had to brief the new chairman, Sir Stuart Burgess, and CEO of the Anglia and Oxford regional office, Barbara Stocking. Fortunately, Paul Kemp became the new regional finance director, and Peter Houghton the director of strategy, so there were two former East Anglian regional board members in the new set up familiar with our scheme.

We decided to appoint one of the major consultancy companies to help us with our new, more complicated business case, which had to comply with a much more onerous set of rules, issued by the Treasury in June 1994, to govern NHS capital investment decisions.

We appointed Ernst & Young, and the theme of this latest case was Papworth's strong growth, which over the past five years had seen us double the number of inpatients, from 4,258 to 9,446, and increase our turnover from £9.2m to £27.8m. We managed to reduce the capital cost of our preferred option to £19.3 million, and submitted this revised business case to the regional office in October 1994.

In November 1994, I received a request from the regional office to write a report demonstrating that Papworth's respiratory medical service was truly specialist, and not seeking to attract patients who would normally go to a district general hospital. My colleagues l news

Cambridge Evening News, Monday, November 7, 1994 3

Heart hospital seeks private sector funds

TODAY Wednesday November 9 1994 5

TODAY

EXCLUSIVE

NHS delays funds for crumbling Papworth

in our thoracic directorate, led by Frank Wells as clinical director, provided excellent information describing our pioneering oncology service, pulmonary vascular diseases, respiratory support and sleep centre, and our cystic fibrosis service, showing that we were clearly operating in the specialist area of the respiratory medicine spectrum. We received a reasonably swift confirmation from the regional office that our report answered all their questions, but still there was no answer as to when we could proceed and seek PFI funding.

A couple of months elapsed, and then regional office asked me to provide a second report. This time they wanted a detailed assessment as to how we intended to increase our collaboration with Addenbrooke's Hospital. I suspected that these were delaying tactics being employed by the regional office, whether at their own instigation, or, at the behest of ministers. I complied with this request within one week, and wrote a comprehensive document setting out the existing collaborative arrangements, the range and depth of which, I was later told, surprised them; an example of 'not letting facts get in the way of a good story'. In other words, that they had already made their minds up and decided that Papworth was isolationist and did not co-operate with Addenbrooke's. My report demolished that notion.

I was also able to include details of an initiative with the University of Cambridge School of Clinical Medicine, in the shape of Papworth agreeing to fund a professorial chair in respiratory medicine. This opportunity had arisen in negative circumstances, when John Ashbourne rang to tell me that he was going to set up a respiratory medical service, citing the irregular attendance of Papworth's consultant chest physicians at their Addenbrooke's sessions. Whilst I soon found out that there was some truth in John's claims, I could not help but think there was an element of retaliation, as I had beaten him to the punch in securing the transfer of the former Assisted Ventilation Unit from Newmarket Hospital 18 months earlier.

I lost no time in contacting Keith Peters, and asked him to persuade John Ashbourne not to put their money into a service development, but instead channel it into a professorial chair. I promised to match the funds, as I was keen to stop Addenbrooke's setting up a rival service, which would severely weaken Papworth's financial position and could render our business case for redevelopment unviable. I also contacted Dr Ron Zimmern, the director of public health, at our host commissioner, the Cambridge and Huntingdon Health Commission.

I told Ron that the commissioners would incur additional costs due to the 'supply induced demand' that would inevitably arise, and said that we should instead use this as an opportunity to take forward the academic agenda. My tactics worked, and over the following weeks the establishment of an academic department of respiratory medicine was firmed up, culminating in the appointment of, or in university parlance, the 'election' of a 'Professor of Respiratory Medicine'.

As the person appointed would carry out some direct patient care at Addenbrooke's, and with my promise to ensure that my Papworth consultants would in future turn up on time for their outpatient clinics, it was a win-win outcome.

Well, almost.

At the interview, Papworth's representative, Frank Wells, had faithfully reflected the views of his chest physician colleagues, and this contributed to an 'outside' candidate securing the position. As this was not the outcome that Keith Peters had envisaged, he was soon on the phone asking if Papworth could find the money to fund a second professorial chair, for the local candidate, excellent though he was, came runner-up.

After securing the support of Frank Wells, and my chest physicians, I obtained board approval to fund a second chair in respiratory medicine, principally on the grounds that it would prevent Addenbrooke's setting up a rival service.

This proved to be the case for the next 15 years, but I know that the funding of two professorial chairs beyond 2010 would be questioned by my colleagues at Papworth, so I was pleased to leave that in the 'pending' tray, as they used to say, for my successor!

Two months later, in March 1995, the regional office signalled their satisfaction with this second piece of additional assurance. They hinted that I should receive news on our scheme shortly.

I was angry, therefore, to then receive a request for a third report, this time asking for a paper on the "strategic intent of our research aspirations". When I reminded them of the academic developments in respiratory medicine, they said they needed more evidence of our proposals for cardiac services.

I requested a meeting with the Regius Professor of Physic, Professor Sir Keith Peters, and we met with his colleagues Professor Patrick Sissons and Professor Peter Weissberg. We agreed to draft a paper which included outline thoughts on the establishment of a chair in cardiac surgery, and the concept of a virtual research centre, i.e. investing in staff at Papworth and Cambridge over the next five years. The letter to me from Sir Keith summarising the outcome of this meeting contained the following key points:

> *"The University appreciates the moves made to have a non-executive director drawn from the Clinical School (notwithstanding that the Trust's Establishing Order does not contain this requirement) and this is a key signal of the willingness for both parties to work closely […] Were the School and Papworth to create a joint research centre under a committee or board of management this would report to the Faculty Board and Papworth and be officially recognised in that way […] This is a concept that should be discussed further between us and links with your proposals for a Research and Education Institute. With regard to this, I should like to explore*

further with you building on the strengths in health services and the ways in which academic cardiac surgery might be developed."

Papworth's management executive group had first suggested the idea of an academic department of cardiac surgery in 1992, so I was pleased that this idea had now been accepted, albeit only in principle, by the Regius Professor.

This third report was submitted to the regional office in early April 1995.

A few days later, I received confirmation that Prime Minister John Major had accepted my invitation to come to Papworth to officially open the final two of the six significant capital projects completed in the past couple of years, a fourth operating theatre, and additional intensive care beds.

During the visit in late April, Mr Major asked me how things were progressing with the redevelopment. He was taken aback when I told him of the delays caused by the seemingly endless requests for further information or clarification. He said I should write to him at the House of Commons, giving him a brief résumé of recent experiences, and he "would look into it."

I wasted little time in firing off a letter to him, quoting the three pieces of additional information I had been asked to provide to the regional office before they would let us move forward by approving our outline business case (OBC). I received an acknowledgement from his constituency secretary, Gina Hearn, after only

Prime Minister John Major meeting patients

nine days, who, according to protocol, promised to keep our MP, Sir Anthony Grant, fully in the picture.

In early July, I received two further letters from Gina Hearn. The first letter confirmed that Mr Major "*did raise your concerns with the Secretary of State, and he has asked me to forward to you the reply he has now received from Mrs Bottomley, which he hopes will serve to reassure you about the consideration being given to your proposals.*"

The letter in question, from Virginia Bottomley, written on 28th June read:

> *"Mr Bridge's frustration at what must seem to him to be an unacceptable wait is appreciated. However, any project of the size proposed by Papworth needs the most thorough scrutiny before it can be given the go-ahead. It is not just a question of the available money, and I believe that this is not the issue here."*

In fact I knew that the secretary of state had previously spelt out her preference for Papworth to move to Cambridge, as she had written as such to Sir Terence English during their correspondence about the future of Guy's Hospital, London. Terence had kindly told me this a few weeks earlier. However, she could not be seen to be at odds with her prime minister.

Having put my head above the parapet, I expected a phone call from the regional office admonishing me for my actions. Instead, the summer passed with only a few enquiries into the robustness of our clinical activity projections. Regular telephone contact between Gina Hearn and myself resulted in a further letter from me to the prime minister in late August, in which I said that matters had "not progressed". Stephen Dorrell, the new secretary of state, must have been contacted by the prime minister's office, and he replied as follows:

> *"I appreciate Mr Bridge's frustration at what must seem to him to be an unacceptable wait. However, any project of the size proposed by Papworth needs the most thorough scrutiny before it can be approved."*

Thus far the letter was a repeat of the one two months earlier from Virginia Bottomley, no doubt drafted by the same civil servant. The difference was that this latest letter offered hope that a decision would be made in October 1995.

On 26th September, I was asked to attend a meeting of the Supra Regional Services Advisory Committee, as they would be considering our business case in their capacity as our second largest purchaser, representing 17% of Papworth's income. This Department of Health's 'arm's-length body' was the 'purchaser' of highly specialised clinical services, which in Papworth's case meant heart and lung transplants. The politics of this meeting, I was later told, was to find a way of supporting Papworth's plans, but not setting a precedent and departing from the official Department of Health line of encouraging single specialty hospitals to amalgamate with their teaching hospital compatriots. They were particularly keen not to give any encouragement to the 'Save Harefield Hospital' campaign which had recently been launched, no doubt inspired by the successful Papworth campaign. Following my attendance at this meeting, I received a very positive letter, the key paragraph being as follows:

> *"During the discussion, it was explained that the option of moving your unit to Addenbrooke's had been carefully considered and found to be impractical and that no other obvious unit Papworth could merge with was apparent. In these circumstances, the group decided that, whilst recognising that developments in transplantation may mean that providing such a service on a single specialty site is likely to become increasingly unsatisfactory, it was prepared to support the Papworth proposal to redevelop on its existing site and would continue to purchase the service for as long as it continued to meet the necessary quality and price standards. In reaching this view, the group expressed the hope that the close collaborative working referred to above would continue and develop."*

This was an incredibly important letter, and I hoped that our other main purchasers would now feel able to follow suit and give their approval to our case for redeveloping our existing site at Papworth Everard.

Eventually, on 30th October, which happened to be my 40th birthday, I received a letter from the regional office approving our OBC, allowing us to proceed to 'final' business case stage, and seek expressions of interest from potential PFI partners. The letter concluded:

> *"I am pleased therefore to confirm regional office approval for the trust Outline Business Case at a capital cost of £20,518."*

On 14th November, I received a letter from the prime minister congratulating me on getting the go-ahead. It was a very kind gesture, and totally unexpected.

Another consultant appointment panel which sticks in my memory took place in 1995. The interview was for another chest physician, but this time with specific responsibility for patients being assessed for heart and lung transplants, and their follow-up care. The role had been carried out for the previous two years, with great distinction, by Keith McNeil, an Australian, who was the latest doctor to come from that country and work at Papworth, for a fixed two-year period, and gain experience in heart and lung transplant medicine.

John Wallwork asked me if we could establish a permanent post, which the board readily agreed to, and we were very pleased that Keith McNeil applied for this

From: The Rt Hon John Major MP

Attachment 2

HOUSE OF COMMONS
LONDON SW1A 0AA

14 November 1995

Dear Stephen

I was delighted to hear that Papworth's redevelopment has now been given the green light.

I know how frustrating the wait has been for you all but I hope that the redevelopment will now be able to proceed without further delay.

With best wishes

Yours sincerely

John

S J Bridge Esq
Chief Executive
Papworth Hospital NHS Trust
Papworth Everard
Cambridge CB3 8RE

role, prepared to swap Brisbane and the Gold Coast for the Cambridgeshire fens!

Audrey Stenner once again chaired the panel, and there were three candidates to interview. Following the questions from the six medical members and me, Audrey said that she had a question for Keith. She then asked him if any of his ancestors might have been convicts, transported from Britain a couple of hundred years ago!

John Wallwork nudged me in the ribs and said, "Are you going to let her get away with that?" But before I had a chance to say anything, Keith leaned back in his chair, stretched out his six-foot eight-inch frame, and said, "Gee, Audrey, I guess I never thought about that."

Keith was appointed, and played an important role in the development of several clinical initiatives for the next six years until he returned to Brisbane, where he enjoyed a successful transition into health management. In 2009, at John Wallwork's birthday party, held in his garden, I introduced Keith, in the UK on holiday, to Andrew Lansley, who was then the shadow secretary of state for health, and said, "Andrew, this is the type of chap we need more of in NHS management," and left them to discuss the merits of their respective health services. Little did I imagine that Keith would return to Cambridge a few years later to become the CEO of Cambridge University Hospitals.

CHAPTER TEN

1996

This Wasn't in the Job Description

My colleagues and I wasted little time in moving the process forward, initially by advertising in the *Official Journal of the European Union (OJEU)*, seeking partners in the PFI. A briefing day was held in January 1996, and of the 27 companies who attended, 10 submitted an Expression of Interest. Following evaluation, we selected three companies to submit outline bids, from which we then selected two bidders to go into the final stage. The final two were Sir Robert McAlpine and HCDA Chesterton. As the months of 1996 passed, it became obvious that the cost of their proposals far exceeded the £20.5 million authorised by the regional office.

The first three months of 1996 were memorable for me, but for entirely negative reasons. I was informed in the previous September that the widower of a deceased transplant patient had made threats to kill staff at Papworth and Addenbrooke's. He was unhappy at the events surrounding her death, and although he now lived in southwest England, 30 years earlier he had been a member of the Kray gang in London. I arranged to meet Mr R, and was accompanied by Dr Jayan Parameshwar, the consultant in overall charge of this lady's care. We met in my office on 11th October 1995, during which Mr R demanded to meet all of the doctors involved in his late wife's care, including John Wallwork, the transplant director. If this did not happen, he said there would be 'a bloodbath'. I said I would set about organising a meeting with the senior doctors and other key clinical staff, and he promised to give me some dates in early January 1996.

After the meeting, I informed the local police, who were aware of previous events in this matter. They asked to be kept informed of any developments, but said they could do nothing else at this time. After several difficult telephone conversations with Mr R, he and I agreed on a date for the meeting, 15th January. Mr R had arranged a meeting at Addenbrooke's involving their CEO, John Ashbourne, and the relevant doctors, at 10.30am that day, so the meeting at Papworth was scheduled for 12.30pm.

A couple of days before the meeting, the police informed me that they would have armed police in an unmarked car, positioned in the petrol station about one mile from Papworth, and they would contact me when Mr R's Range Rover passed by.

At 1pm on the 15th I received a telephone call from John Ashbourne, who told me their meeting had overrun, but they felt that they had satisfied Mr R's grievances, so he wished me good luck. At 1.30pm, John Wallwork, who had been on standby to attend the meeting, said he could wait no longer as he had a difficult operation to perform at a neighbouring hospital, and left the site. *Thanks, John,* I thought, *you owe me one!*

About 1.45pm the police rang to tell me that Mr R had passed the petrol station, and should be with us in a few minutes. They added that I should tell them if Mr R was carrying a bag, as it might contain a gun. That comment did not help to settle my nerves.

Mr R was accompanied by a lady, who he introduced as his secretary, and was a calming influence, he added, to prevent his volatile temper erupting. Mr R did have a carrier bag, but it thankfully contained nothing more sinister than his packed lunch. Having explained that they had got lost after leaving Addenbrooke's, the meeting started, and I asked several clinical colleagues to join us, one at a time, to answer Mr R's questions.

After the end of the second interview, Audrey Stenner, our chairman, joined the meeting to give me some moral support, as she knew how difficult the previous few months had been for me. Audrey had a lot of experience dealing with irate parents during her time as headmistress of a primary school, but nothing had prepared her for Mr R's verbal onslaught towards her, full of profanities. Audrey gladly took my advice and left the room. Towards the end of the third interview, Mr R was getting tired, and became irritable, and finally snapped and said that if he did not get better answers then "there would be a lot of dead bodies around Papworth, so there would no shortage of donor organs!"

At this point I adjourned the meeting, and Mr R's secretary took him outside and calmed him down. We agreed to meet again in a couple of weeks, when Mr R had studied the detailed written information we had prepared for him.

Back in my office, Audrey and I agreed that this situation needed to be brought to a mutually agreeable solution. I decided to speak with our consultant histopathologist, Dr Nat Cary, who was also a Home Office pathologist, and had extensive contacts with the police. Nat said he would speak to a local superintendent, who was very experienced in these sorts of matters.

I soon got a telephone call from Superintendent R, coincidentally the same surname as Mr R, and a tape machine was installed in my office. Over the next few weeks, my telephone calls with Mr R were taped – and the full unexpurgated version, full of further threats to Papworth including, for the first time, myself, were typed up by my loyal personal assistant, Barbara Gamble. During one of our latter telephone conversations, I told Mr R that I would be away from the office for a few days, as my wife was due to give birth to our third child. His response, at first, seemed sincere, wishing me all the best, but then followed up by telling me that my office was very exposed, and if he did not get the answers he wanted that "one night you could be sitting there at your desk, and boom! the next minute, you're gone."

Two other telephone conversations I had with Mr R, which chilled my blood at the time, took place on the 20th and 25th March.

During the first exchange, I said I would arrange for an independent enquiry into the care of his late wife. He thanked me, but then said, "Everyone has been dragging their feet hoping I would go away. You are wrong if that's what you think. What happened at that kiddies' school[6] is nothing to what will happen if I don't get some answers."

Then, during our final conversation on 25th March, Mr R said, "Look, I'll give you a week to phone me back and confirm that the doctors have agreed to meet with me. Otherwise it will be too bloody late, I'll tell you that straight. I don't care how many police officers are listening; I couldn't care two hoots, 'cos if I don't get to you I have someone who will. I appreciate what you've done, but it's about time you dug bloody Wallwork out and made him do something, 'cos he knows more about this. I'll give you till the end of next week and then I'll come down , but I'm not sure if I'm going to bring my guns.

"The only way in life to settle your grievances is to deal with them head on. I've been brought up the hard way. I lived in Elephant and Castle[7], and worked for the Krays and Richardsons years ago, so I am not about to be put down easily. I will come back. The only way they will stop me is if they shoot me stone-dead in your bloody

---

6 He was referring the horrific shootings in Dunblane, Scotland.

7 A suburb in south London.

hospital. But I tell you now, if that happens, that won't be the end of it, because the other side of my family still runs south London, and they will come and get you.

"And another thing I'll tell you, I 've been walking at Breezy Head and the local police have been taking photos of me. I'm not bloody happy about that. I will shoot them so fucking dead, I'll tell you that straight. I tell you, Mr Bridge, the way I feel, for Christ's sake, is that you have to do something before it's too fucking late."

Within a week, after studying the transcripts of our telephone calls, police from Cambridgeshire travelled to Mr R's home in the southwest and arrested him. He was brought to Huntingdon police station, where he was charged but released on bail, with conditions of not contacting Papworth or returning to this county.

One month later, Mr R pleaded guilty to the various charges and was given a 12-month prison sentence, suspended for two years. After the verdict, the court was told that Mr R had a track record of threatening hospitals in his own area which had previously treated his late wife.

In the summer of 1996, I met the new prospective Conservative parliamentary candidate, following Sir Anthony Grant's decision to retire at the next election. His name was Andrew Lansley, and he went on to become health secretary in 2010.

As 1996 drew to a close, my colleagues and I made several changes to the two designs prepared by HCDA Chesterton and Robert McAlpine in an attempt to get close to the sum approved by the regional office. Our two bidders

Audrey Stenner, Stephen Bridge, and recently elected constituency MP Andrew Lansley

naïvely believed that because of the prime minister's interest in this scheme, the budget could be exceeded.

Tensions between my chairman and I continued, as the Sir Robert McAlpine design was clearly her preferred choice; but the cost was £13 million (65%) over budget, as they had disregarded the brief for a partial redevelopment, and instead gone for a 'greenfield' option on neighbouring land, which we did not own. I argued in vain that selecting their greenfield option at Papworth laid us open to the charge that we were ignoring the value-for-money benefits offered by partial redevelopment, and potentially wasting much of the circa £7 million of capital improvements we had secured over the previous five years.

A couple of the non-executives told me to "watch my back", as Audrey and her two closest non-executives were not happy with my stance on this matter.

CHAPTER ELEVEN

1997-99

The Move to Cambridge: The Lady is Not For Turning, or is She?

At our January 1997 board meeting, a particularly stressful one I seem to recall, the Sir Robert McAlpine greenfield option, costing £33 million, was selected by the casting vote of the chairman. I had allowed my executive director colleagues a free vote, and one of them voted to support the McAlpine option.

The next day, our university NED, Professor Sir Dillwyn Williams, resigned, and this received prominent coverage in the Sunday newspapers.

Over the next four months I negotiated further cost reductions to the McAlpine option, and got the sum down to circa £27 million. However, this resulted in an awkward, split-site design, and before we had a chance to test its effectiveness, the General Election had resulted in a landslide victory for New Labour and Tony Blair.

Top doctor quits in hospital funding row

Private cash wrong for patients and trusts, Papworth chief warns minister

Sir Dillwyn Williams: Government 'overplaying benefits'

About one week after the new government took office, I was informed by the regional office that all work must be halted on PFI schemes, as they were to be subjected to a government review. We were asked to complete a detailed pro forma, assessing appropriateness and cost effectiveness, and also offered the opportunity to meet with ministers to discuss the merits of our scheme.

I asked our new MP, Andrew Lansley, to accompany me to a meeting at Department of Health headquarters at Richmond House, Whitehall, to meet with Alan Milburn, the number two to Secretary of State, Frank Dobson, and the minister with responsibility for the hospital sector. Andrew and I spent a convivial 45 minutes with Alan Milburn, making our case as to why the Papworth project was important and should be allowed to proceed. I recall the friendly banter between the two, as the new minister joked about the tasteless black leather sofas he had inherited from his Tory predecessor, Gerry Malone.

Despite our special pleading, I was informed several weeks later that our scheme would not be allowed to proceed. I then received a phone call from Barbara Stocking, the regional director, who advised me that the only 'show in town' was to pursue relocation to Cambridge on the Addenbrooke's site.

I now feared a return to the spectre of uncertainty about our whole future, but concluded that given the slow pace of change in the NHS we would still be at Papworth in ten years' time. For the safety of patients, we needed to continue our campaign to replace the old, worn-out estate, particularly in clinical areas, where the 1930s buildings offered little or no dignity for our patients, and in our 45-bed timber-framed cardiac block, which posed a potential fire hazard.

I asked our estate's advisers to draw up plans for three projects: to replace the cardiac block, to build an extension to the very successful RSSC, and thirdly, build a dedicated cardiology day case unit. I was determined to send out a message that Papworth was still strong, bustling with ideas and refusing to give up, despite this serious blow.

In view of the likelihood of a move to Cambridge now looking to be the only option, I was conscious that we must not be seen to 'waste taxpayers' money' and go for the more expensive permanent buildings, if temporary-type buildings would suffice at a significantly lower cost. We therefore decided to pursue that route for the RSSC extension and a cardiology day ward, but it was not feasible for the replacement 45-bed cardiac ward block.

Despite the usual, predictable reservations of our host Health Authority (Cambridge and Huntingdon) about supporting further capital investment at Papworth, I obtained the approval of our regional Capital Planning Group to allow me to spend £1.5 million of our own money replacing the wooden ward block. Thanks, in particular, to the support of the Norfolk and Suffolk Health Authorities, I not only managed to secure the further £0.6 million to allow this scheme to proceed, but also received the group's approval for the two other capital projects, both of which were also to be funded from Papworth's internal monies, £3 million in total.

So much for the 'freedoms' of NHS trusts, I thought, as the pendulum of power had swung firmly into the camp of the 'commissioners', i.e. the purchasing Health Authorities.

Our new medical director, John Wallwork, and I agreed that we needed to engage with Addenbrooke's and explore how their fledgling plan to double the size of their site could help us plan for a relocation of Papworth, in a purpose-designed building. In conjunction with the University of Cambridge, and the Medical Research Council, Addenbrooke's had drafted a strategic plan for their existing 65-acre site, envisaging the acquisition of the adjoining 70 acres. They called this the '20:20 Vision' and, if successful, would transform the fortunes of this campus. This very important document was written by Stephen Davies, a senior manager at Addenbrooke's, who had a forensic ability to analyse complex issues and translate them into information able to be understood by the layperson. Stephen and I were to work together on several projects in the future, most notably the formation of the Academic Health Science Centre, which we called Cambridge University Health Partners. Once again, Stephen's brilliant intellect and excellent briefing papers were crucial factors in us achieving designation of this flagship enterprise.

The year closed with a meeting in a smart hotel near Norwich, which John Wallwork and I agreed to attend to discuss the future of cardiac surgery in the east of England. The meeting had been requested by the chief executive of the Norfolk and Norwich Hospital, Malcolm Stamp, a very experienced CEO who had previously worked in the politically charged northwest region, accompanied by his former thoracic surgeon, Barry Ross, who was now one of his non-executive directors.

This meeting was to have a bizarre and totally unexpected outcome.

I was not looking forward to this meeting for two reasons. First, when Malcolm and I had met soon after his appointment in 1994, he made it very clear that he would get cardiac surgery at Norwich, with or without Papworth's support. His exact words to me at that meeting were, "You seem like a nice bloke, but if we can't do a deal, well, then I will ****ing stuff you." I wasn't offended, as I had several NHS friends in Manchester and Liverpool, and they told me that Malcolm often conducted business in such a robust manner, and it was not personal, it was just his style.

The other reason I was not looking forward to this meeting was that I had offended Barry Ross with the wording of our trust application document in 1992, when I said that Papworth "would work closely with Norfolk and Norwich Hospital upon the impending retirement of their senior thoracic surgeon." He subsequently rang to berate me for putting into print something that was not public knowledge, and would have a disastrous impact on his referrals. I apologised, and our paths had not crossed until now.

The meeting took place over supper and, after exchanging pleasantries, we were less than halfway through the main course when Malcolm asked Barry to set out his hopes for cardiac surgery at Norwich.

Over the next five minutes, Barry waxed lyrical over the excellence of Papworth Hospital, a jewel in the NHS crown, and how nothing should be done to jeopardise Papworth's future. I could have fallen off my chair, and tried not to look at Malcolm's face. After some further discussion on wider NHS issues, the meeting came to a close. Barry Ross gave his apologies, and left for another engagement, closely followed by Malcolm Stamp. Although accommodation had been arranged for John Wallwork and me, John said he would prefer to sleep in his own bed; and because I had arranged a meeting in Great Yarmouth the next morning, I retired to my room several hours earlier than I had expected.

It was to be four years before Malcolm raised the subject again.

The year 1998 began with me getting plans drawn up for the replacement of another unsuitable building, our pathology laboratory. The 'temporary' facilities which the pathology laboratory had occupied for decades was now totally unsuitable, and Clinical Director, Dr Susan Stewart, pushed hard for a replacement building for this essential service.

We had also decided to celebrate the 50th anniversary of the NHS by having a dedicated building for the fast-expanding transplant service to replace the 'temporary' facility which we had acquired at the beginning of the decade.

In May 1998, the regional office asked me to work with Director of Public Health for Cambridge and Huntingdon Health Authority, Dr Ron Zimmern, to undertake an assessment of the needs for specialist cardiothoracic services in the eastern region over the next ten years.

The result of our collaboration was a 17-page report which came out in favour of Papworth moving to a greenfield site adjacent to Addenbrooke's. Our report did not consider whether a second centre would be required, given that the southern part of the region (Essex, Hertfordshire and south Bedfordshire) referred their patients to hospitals in London – namely the Royal Brompton, Harefield, Barts and University College Hospital.

The year 1999 saw ministers make further changes to the boundaries of the regional and district tiers of NHS management. A new eastern regional office was formed which, losing the former Oxford 'arm', moved its headquarters back to Cambridge, only five years after moving to Milton Keynes. A new Cambridgeshire Health Authority, incorporating Peterborough, also came into existence on 1st April.

Little time was lost by these new organisations in launching a strategic review of the acute hospital and community service provision needed in the fast-growing county of Cambridgeshire, whose population was predicted to increase by 40%, to one million over the next 20 years.

The blueprint for the future, setting out a summary of the new facilities that would be required, was unveiled in September 1999. This contained a shopping list of £400 million in capital investment, and formed the basis of what was to become a new hospital for Peterborough, and day case centres for Addenbrooke's and Hinchingbrooke hospitals. The document also reiterated the importance of Papworth moving to Cambridge onto a greenfield site adjacent to Addenbrooke's, and called on the government to remove the greenbelt designation to allow this to happen.

The position of Papworth's chairman, Audrey Stenner, was still one of vehement opposition to a move to Cambridge, saying in one board meeting that it would happen "over my dead body". This was despite all the evidence showing that no government would invest a very large sum of money for facilities in a relatively isolated, rural location, such as Papworth Everard.

Her stance caused John Wallwork and me problems in attempting to negotiate the best deal for Papworth in what otherwise was an exciting time for the NHS, as significant additional investment had been promised by the Blair government.

So, in the summer of 1999, having served seven years and two terms as chairman, I suggested to Regional Director, Peter Houghton, that any offer to Audrey for a third term should be for a shorter period, but which

Cambridge Evening News

The Award Winning Voice of Mid-Anglia

WEDNESDAY, SEPTEMBER 22, 1999 PRICE: 32p

300 JOBS IN OUR 24-PAGE PULLOUT / TOKEN SEVEN IN OUR SHOPPING SPREE CONTEST – PAGE 17

2007 DEADLINE ON PAPWORTH MOVE

£400m plan to cope with booming population

PAPWORTH Hospital looks set to move to the Addenbrooke's site by 2007 – ending years of debate about the future of the leading chest and heart centre.

The news came as a £400 million development strategy to cope with the expected population boom in Cambridge was announced by Cambridgeshire Health Authority.

The strategy, which lays out a framework for expansion over the next 20 years, says moving Papworth to Addenbrooke's will benefit patients by eliminating 14-mile ambulance journeys for patients who need to be transferred, and pooling world-class research expertise on one site.

By CLARE YOUELL

Stephen Bridge, Papworth's chief executive, said: "Over the years we have spent a great deal of time and money examining in detail all possible solutions regarding our future."

He said patients and staff had "understandable misgivings" about moving, but the hospital had to look at what was best for patients in the future.

The first open heart surgery was carried out at Papworth 41 years ago. It now performs around 1,500 open heart operations each year, and about 100 transplants.

The hospital, which has 206 beds serving 2.4 million people, has seen its workload increase by 300 per cent over the last decade. Over the next 10 years, it will need at least 60 more beds to cater for 30,000 more patients.

The strategy also includes:

■ Developing the Addenbrooke's site into a world-class South Cambridge Biomedical Campus with new access routes, landscaping and parking.

■ Boosting GP-led community services and intermediate care.

■ Investing in one-stop clinics and using modern technology to send patient data to hospitals by computer link.

Addenbrooke's and Hinchingbrooke hospitals have drawn up their own development plans, which will be released in the next few weeks.

The strategy includes expansion of Addenbrooke's Hills Road site, to improve teaching and research facilities, access and parking, and possibly a railway station at Long Road.

Roy Male, Addenbrooke's chief executive, said: "If we cannot develop the site, we will not be able to look after the extra people.

"Pooling the outstanding resources of Papworth and Addenbrooke's on a single site will be of enormous benefit to patients at both hospitals."

Hinchingbrooke Hospital in Huntingdon would also be upgraded to enable it to cope with its anticipated 40,000 share of the extra population.

The expected population explosion of up to 150,000 over the next 20 years is the equivalent of treating a city the size of Cambridge, and two towns the size of Huntingdon.

Coun Geoff Heathcock, Liberal Democrat health spokesman, said parking problems at Addenbrooke's needed to be addressed before any expansion plans could work.

■ Cambridgeshire Health Authority has revealed plans to move its HQ from its Cambridge and Peterborough offices to Huntingdon. Work started this week on the site at Hinchingbrooke Business Park.

■ Opinion – Page 8

could be extended if she helped bring about a resolution to the Papworth issue by acknowledging that a greenfield site in Cambridge was now the only option on the table.

Peter and his chair, Rosie Varley, must have advised Audrey to modify her position, as she was awarded a third term of two years.

The government had recently launched its National Service Framework for Heart Disease, and it pledged to cut premature deaths by increasing the number of procedures/operations carried out, and thereby slashing waiting times. Significant money for additional staff and facilities was promised and, despite the uncertainty about our long-term future, I was determined to grab as much of this government money as I could to improve the lot of the three million people in East Anglia who looked to Papworth for these specialist services. I submitted business cases for a new intensive care unit, and more cardiac catheterisation suites. These turned out to be the last business cases I would write, as the NHS subsequently changed the rules and made them ostensibly into financial documents, devoid of a lot of their clinical content, to be replaced by masses of spreadsheets. I bowed out on a high, and was delighted when our bid for £7 million capital was approved.

I was particularly pleased with the business case I wrote for a new intensive care unit of 26 beds, which took up most of my Sunday mornings in my office, in the summer of 1999.This was a more productive way of working as the hospital was quiet, but I was still kept 'in the know', as several clinical colleagues would pop in for a coffee.

I was to present the business case to the Regional Capital Steering Group, chaired by Malcolm Stamp, the indomitable CEO of the Norfolk and Norwich Hospital. I decided to use the tactic of 'a picture tells a thousand words', so asked my nursing colleagues in the small ICU to move as much medical equipment in there as was possible, and to be photographed by Graham, the hospital's audio visual technician, hoping to show a cluttered and cramped environment in which to treat very sick patients. The photographs turned out fine, and only five minutes into my presentation, Malcolm interjected and said, "These pictures are a disgrace. How can Steve and his team provide top quality care in these appalling conditions?" Malcolm then proposed that my business case be approved in full, which it was, unanimously, by the dozen members, and I left the room hugely relieved and very grateful to Malcolm for his intervention.

The opinion of some senior figures at Addenbrooke's and the Cambridgeshire Health Authority towards me at this time was that I was not serious about pursuing a move to Cambridge, since I was busily building at Papworth.

My logic was simple.

The government was in a hurry to deliver on its promises to significantly improve the provision of cardiac and cancer care, and, in the case of the former, Papworth was the only hospital which could deliver their agenda within the timescales they demanded. Furthermore, my intuition told me that it would take several years before the greenbelt designation in Cambridge would be lifted. That, together with the urgent need to expand hospitals in Peterborough, Cambridge and Huntingdon in view of the impending rapid population growth, would see Papworth's case slip down the priority list. I concluded, therefore, that Papworth would remain in its present location for at least a decade, i.e. until 2009, so to do nothing and not to push for new facilities would be irresponsible.

From the mid-1990s, the government became very concerned about the possible implications of the 'Millennium Bug', and in particular whether serious harm could be inflicted on patients in the NHS by the malfunctioning of the vast amount of medical and scientific equipment with computer chips in them. The director of planning for the NHS, one Alasdair Liddell, toured the country urging senior NHS managers to take this matter seriously.

In 1997, the director of our Anglia and Oxford region, Barbara Stocking, had asked me to chair a group to assess the readiness of all the NHS organisations in this area. I managed to meet with all the chief executives of the Health Authorities and trusts over the next 12 months, and, assisted by staff from the regional office, produce an organisational audit report setting out where we felt that more work was necessary. I handed over the chairmanship to the new regional office, established for eastern England in early 1999, as the Department of Health understandably wanted these new organisations to be responsible for this topic as the 31st December approached.

I saw in the new millennium in my office at Papworth. Together with Kate Lancaster, my head of communications, we toured the wards and handed out good quality pens or tasteful glass paperweights to the staff working on this historic night. When we had finished, I returned to my office, and thought that I would go home at 3am, assuming that if any of our equipment was to malfunction, then it would have happened by now. At 2.30am, Paul Robbins, our head of medical electronics, came to my office to tell me he had found a fault on a piece of equipment, which, whilst not playing up for 1st January, would, however, not work on 29th February 2000. Feeling somewhat embarrassed, given my previous chairmanship of the region wide group, I told Paul to contact the team at the Department of Health, and report this 'leap year fault'. I was delighted when he rang me one hour later, telling me that the DH hotline was playing a recorded message saying that no one was available: they had apparently gone home at 3am, as no one had contacted them with any reports of malfunctioning equipment!

CHAPTER TWELVE

2000

Making Headlines

In January 2000, I was asked by Barbara Stocking, now regional director of the southeast region, to lead an enquiry into a high-profile claim by a whistle-blower of management failings at the Oxford Heart Centre, John Radcliffe Hospital. A senior nurse had alleged that patients had been harmed due to the personal and professional shortcomings of some of the senior medical team in the cardiac unit, and that management were trying to cover it up. As a result of her claims, a brick was thrown through her window, and the story made the front page of *The Sunday Times*.

Before I could start the Oxford review, I became embroiled in a major media story about deaths on the waiting list for cardiac surgery at Papworth. This time the reaction of the Department of Health press office was completely different to that of 1991, when I was splashed across the front page of *The Daily Mirror*.

I received several telephone calls from senior colleagues at the regional office, telling me that the prime minister's Special Adviser', Alistair Campbell, was very angry at what he perceived to be briefing against the government by John Wallwork and myself.

Nothing was further from the truth, but whilst John was probably immune from retribution, I was informed that I was not.

The matter was resolved after five days, when it was agreed that Junior Health Minister, Lord Philip Hunt, would ring Audrey Stenner. Since Audrey's reappointment for a third term commenced a few months earlier, our working relationship had improved enormously as she came to terms with the inevitability of our move to Cambridge. Audrey was given the choice of taking this important phone call at work or at home, which seemed ominous. She chose the latter, telling me that if she was to be fired, she would prefer to receive the news in her armchair, with a glass of whisky beside her. When the call eventually came, Lord Hunt used first names, and mentioned that he remembered Audrey from his time as CEO of the National Association of Health Authorities and Trusts. He advised her to tell me to keep a low profile for a few months.

I apologised to Audrey for placing her in a difficult position, and we agreed that Papworth would refuse to do interviews on potentially controversial topics, and ensure that future press releases would concentrate on purely clinical matters.

BBC HOMEPAGE | WORLD SERVICE | EDUCATION   low graphics version | feedback | help

BBC NEWS

You are in: Health

Front Page
World
UK
UK Politics
Business
Sci/Tech
Health
Medical notes
Background
Briefings
Education
Sport
Entertainment
Talking Point
In Depth
AudioVideo

Wednesday, 15 March, 2000, 19:29 GMT

'60 patients died waiting for surgery'

Papworth needs more intensive care beds

A leading heart hospital says 60 patients died waiting for surgery last year.

Surgeons at Papworth Hospital in Cambridgeshire say more intensive care beds could have saved lives and have asked the government for £5m to build a new wing.

They want to bring waiting times down to three months, but there are currently 2,000 people waiting for heart treatment.

> "Because there is an element of risk in heart treatment, patients will die waiting"
>
> **John Wallwork, Papworth Hospital**

John Wallwork, medical director at the hospital, which is the heart and lung specialist centre for East Anglia, said demand was rising faster than resources.

The government has made heart surgery one of it key priorities for the NHS and has allocated an extra £50m to tackle the crisis. But critics say this is a drop in the ocean.

Chief executive at the hospital Stephen Bridge admitted staff had a "massive job to do" to cut the backlog for diagnosis and surgery.

He told the BBC: "It is acknowledged by the medical profession that some patients would have still been alive if they had got their treatment earlier.

"Here is a very effective treatment and this country lags behind the rest of western Europe. We have a massive job on our hands."

Mr Wallwork: "Patients die waiting"

Dr Wallwork added: "It is very frustrating when we can't help all the people we could.

"The problem is demand has been rising and the demand is more than we can deal with with our resources and because there is an element of risk in heart treatment, patients will die waiting."

One patient, Billy Rushmere, waited 13 months for surgery and is now preparing to go home.

He said he was one of the lucky ones because he was able to live a virtually normal life before his treatment. Other were not so lucky.

The hospital has yet to hear whether its request for £5m to fund extra intensive care beds has been successful, but Mr Bridge said he was confident he would hear positive news shortly.

On 27th June, Papworth hosted a visit of Dr Roger Boyle, the national director for heart disease, or the 'Heart Tsar', as the media dubbed him. The previous evening I went for a meal with Roger and Peter Schofield, one of our consultant cardiologists. The following morning, I recall taking the receipt for the evening meal out of my wallet and attaching it to my expenses sheet. At lunchtime, I went to the lecture theatre, where Dr Boyle was meeting staff, followed by a buffet lunch and a Q&A session. As the session finished, I noticed that my wallet was not in my trouser pocket, having left my jacket hung up in my office. Neither was the wallet in my jacket and, after searching a few places to no avail, I received a telephone call from my bank. They told me that several cash transactions of £900 had been made in Cambridge, and at the Lakeside Shopping Centre in Essex, and so they had cancelled the offending credit card.

The next day, after being interviewed by a police constable from the local St Neots station, the bank informed me that the amount withdrawn was close to £15,000. The St Neots police then rang me to say they had viewed the CCTV tapes near my office and had a good image of the likely thief, which they planned to send to BBC *Crimewatch*. They added that they were quite excited, as this would be the first time they had featured on this national TV programme.

A couple of weeks later my theft was featured as the final item on *Crimewatch*, and thankfully they saved my blushes by not mentioning whose wallet was stolen. I was never informed if anyone was convicted of this crime, and fortunately my bank wrote off the money stolen.

Between March and September 2000, I spent around two days a week on the Oxford review. My two colleagues were Wilma McPherson and Jules Dussek, the chief nurse and senior thoracic surgeon respectively, from Guy's and St Thomas' Hospital. Jules was absolutely brilliant, with his incisive mind and abundant common sense keeping us focused on the task we were set. As the saying goes, we were 'as welcome as a fart in a space suit', and quite a few of the (mainly medical and management) staff we interviewed seemed to resent our presence. One bizarre interview took place, off site, at the Radcliffe Infirmary in the city centre on a glorious summer's evening. Jules, Wilma and I turned up at 5.30pm, to be met by six consultant anaesthetists dressed in black motorcycle leathers, leaning back in their chairs, looking like half-a-dozen Marlon Brandos in the film *The Wild One*.

I assumed that we were expected to be intimidated, but after a perfunctory 30 minutes of questions we left, with Wilma exclaiming that we had just witnessed something bordering on the 'sexual', although she would not expand on what she meant.

Further interviews took place, including with the senior surgeon Steve Westaby, who did not answer the questions but gave us a lecture on how Oxford was not given the recognition it deserved. As this was the last interview of the day he walked with me to the car park, during which I told him that the world had changed, and that things he and I would have been thanked for in the past – he, for conducting heroic and risky surgery; me, for continuing to use old and unsafe hospital buildings – would now get us fired. I don't think he accepted my point.

I wrote the bulk of the report, with a great deal of assistance from Jules. A phrase that seemed to me to sum up the Oxford scenario came into my head, and it was as follows: "At a time when the NHS is gearing up to implement the NHS plan, Oxford is on its knees, riven with internal conflict . . ." As I thought, this phrase was picked up by the media, with the *Today* programme running it as their main story on the 6am and 7am news the Friday the report was released, before it slipping down the running order.

The Department of Health issued our report along with two other NHS 'bad news' stories on the same day, one Friday in November 2000. A press conference was held at a hotel in Abingdon, several miles away from Oxford, possibly as an attempt to reduce the press interest. The BBC sent their chief health reporter, Niall Dickson, but the combined impact of three 'bad news' NHS stories being issued just before the weekend had the desired effect, and the story died. This was nine months before the infamous 'It's a good day to bury bad news' tactic used by another government department, in the aftermath of the 9/11 outrage.

In May 2000, the first board to board meeting between Addenbrooke's and Papworth took place. This was largely brought about by the diplomacy of our university non-executive, Sir Terence English, who had been appointed Master of St Catharine's College, Cambridge, in 1993, and retired from Papworth in 1995. Following Professor Sir Dlilwyn Williams' resignation, I asked Sir Keith Peters if the university would be comfortable with Terence as their representative on our board. He was positive, but as Audrey Stenner and Terence had not enjoyed the most cordial of relationships during the three years (1992–95), the university pushed the appointment through very quickly before Audrey was in a position to object. However, despite their previous differences, Audrey and Terence worked well together and they came to respect one another during their four years on the board (1997–2001).

The outcome of this board to board meeting was an agreement that the two CEOs and medical directors should work with our counterparts at Cambridgeshire Health Authority to work out the details of what a Papworth on a greenfield site next to Addenbrooke's would consist of, including interactions between the two hospitals. The six of us – Roy Male, David Hardy, Tony Jewell, Alan Burns, John Wallwork and I met several times to progress this work, and the only major disagreement that surfaced between John, myself and the other four was our insistence that we should make provision for future growth in the design of a new Papworth Hospital.

Alan Burns was concerned about this, and gave me the impression that his hidden agenda was to bring about a merger, or more accurately, a takeover of Papworth by Addenbrooke's. I had always believed in the 'form follows function' principle, and knew that if a merger became the official policy of the NHS hierarchy, then it would delay any positive moves on detailed planning for a new Papworth Hospital by years.

After one difficult conversation between John Wallwork and Alan Burns, John told me that Alan had threatened to push through a merger whether we liked it or not. To defuse the situation, I arranged to meet Alan in a pub to propose an idea that Sir Keith Peters, John Wallwork and I had come up with some months earlier.

I suggested to Alan that we should hold a workshop with the key clinicians from the two hospitals, as well as other key stakeholders, and craft a clinical vision for cardiothoracic services for the next 10–15 years, taking the report that Ron Zimmern and I had written two years earlier as a starting point. Emphasising my belief in the 'form follows function' doctrine, I said that this workshop should ban any talk of mergers/takeovers, and get our senior doctors and other clinical staff to channel their energies into designing a clinical service befitting the world-class status of Cambridge. Alan was happy to support this initiative, so I set about organising the workshop, which I planned to hold at Hinxton Hall, south of Cambridge, in April 2001.

CHAPTER THIRTEEN

2001

While the Cat's Away

Late on a Monday evening in mid-January 2001 I had a telephone call from Peter Houghton, the regional director, asking me if I had seen the lurid media coverage of the 'bodies on the floor', at Bedford Hospital mortuary, which the national press were labelling as a national scandal. He then asked if I would be prepared to go to Bedford as a caretaker CEO, to "steady the ship, and keep the doctors on board." Apparently, Alan Milburn, the secretary of state had been summoned to the House of Commons to give an emergency statement, and the region needed a safe pair of hands to be parachuted in whilst the incumbent CEO, my close colleague Ken Williams, was put on 'gardening leave'. I felt I had no option but to agree to Peter's request, subject to the approval of my chairman.

Audrey Stenner acknowledged the gravity of the situation, and agreed to release me. The only condition

Daily Mail

MONDAY, JANUARY 15, 2001

Newspaper of the year

35p

FREE HOROSCOPE FROM DIANA'S ASTROLOGER Token: Page 59

In our Third World NHS, how one hospital treats its dead

THE FINAL INDIGNITY

Mortuary overflow: Bodies are being stored in hospital side room

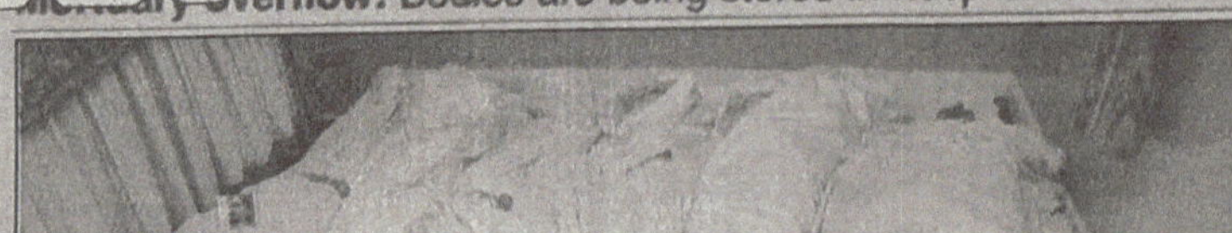

Death room

Bedfordshire on Sunday

Shame of the NHS: How the local newspaper revealed the scandal of the makeshift mortuary in a chapel of rest at Bedford Hospital

The Mirror Monday January 15 2001 www.mirror.co.uk 32p

WIN £1M GUARANTEED TOKEN 10: PAGE 20

SICKENING

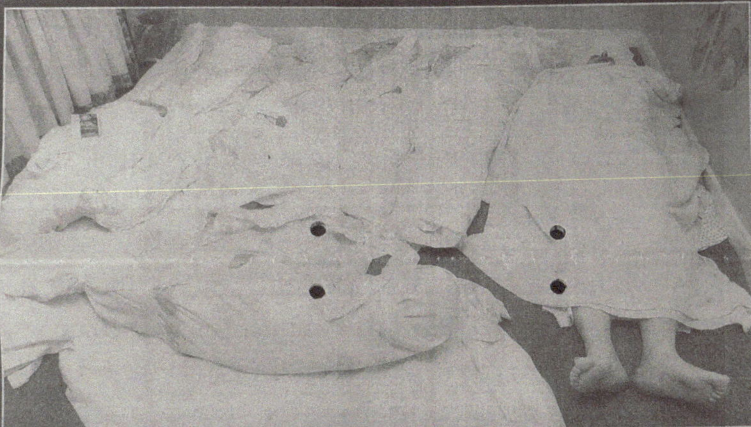

STRIPPED OF DIGNITY: The pathetic row of bodies stored in the hospital chapel – strewn with a couple of fading flowers and next to a rubbish bin in the top left hand corner

Seven bodies lie dumped on a hospital floor, wrapped in sheets .. this is the unforgivable face of the NHS in 2001

By STEPHEN WHITE and FIONA CUMMINS

SEVEN bodies lie bundled up on the floor of an unrefrigerated room at an NHS hospital – lives ending their days in an undignified sprawl on the carpet.

Wrapped in sheets, they were crammed into the chapel at Bedford Hospital for up to 24 hours because the mortuary was full.

Last night, sickened NHS chiefs ordered an inquiry. Local Labour MP Patrick Hall said: "It looks more like a third world hospital."

FULL STORY – PAGE 5

I laid down was to be allowed to continue leading on the future of Papworth Hospital, and the forthcoming Hinxton Hall workshop, which had now grown to 115 delegates.

The media and political interest at Bedford was intense, including a grilling from the BBC's chief health reporter, Niall Dickson, who turned up in my office, unannounced, having persuaded the hospital's inexperienced public relations officer that he only wanted a five-minute chat!

Alan Milburn wanted assurances that there would be no repeat of this episode, and I was bombarded with requests for progress reports. I was relieved when I was told that Paul Kemp, the regional finance director, would lead an investigation into the cause of the 'scandal'. Paul was very experienced at handling politically hot topics, so this now freed me up to try and rebuild relationships, both within Bedford Hospital and among the local community, who felt very bruised by this whole affair.

Things were going well; then, in early April, I was told of another disaster, involving the hospital mortuary. An aborted foetus had been placed in a secure cardboard box and collected by a mortuary attendant from the Pathology Laboratory. Upon his return to the mortuary, he placed the container on top of a wastepaper bin whilst he used the toilet. When he returned the cardboard box was missing, and, for whatever reason, it took several hours before it emerged that a cleaner had disposed of the box in a large skip for domestic waste. The skip had been collected that same day and its contents were deposited in a landfill site in Luton. Despite valiant efforts by several staff searching the site, the box could not be found.

My first duty, I believed, was to contact the parents and to meet with them and personally apologise for this massive error. We met the next day, and the couple were magnanimous, and did not want any member of staff to be disciplined. I, too, felt that way, as the investigation discovered that human error, compounded by insufficient training of staff, and language, were the main causes.

It was only a day later when the local newspaper, *The Beds on Sunday*, contacted me with this story, which I confirmed, and, after apologising, I spelt out the corrective action we had already put in place. They complimented me on my open approach, and although the story was covered by a couple of national papers on the Saturday, there was no repeat of the 'bodies on the floor' media frenzy of two months earlier.

I was particularly pleased to receive the support of the regional organiser of the trade union UNISON, who wrote to the local paper saying, "*I am certain that six months ago the hospital would have handled media enquiries on this matter very differently [...] Your readership should be reassured that Bedford Hospital has improved considerably since the bodies in the chapel scandal, and it continues to do so.*"

I was also pleased to receive support from Peter Houghton, the regional director, and, to my relief, I did not get one phone call from the Department of Health press office.

Several years later, Alan Milburn confirmed to me that the Bedford episode had been one of the catalysts for the foundation trust initiative, as he asked his officials to find a governance model that kept the secretary of state in charge of overall policy, but relieved them of the responsibility of operational matters.

One of the Bedford orthopaedic surgeons, Richard Rawlins, told me that he would be standing as an independent candidate in the forthcoming General Election as a protest against how the hospital had been portrayed in the national media.

One of the reasons I was asked to take over at Bedford was my excellent working relationship with doctors. It was ironic, therefore, that as soon as I had left for Bedford some of the Papworth consultants approached the acting CEO, Stephen Donaldson, and voiced concerns about the proposal to create a chair in cardiac surgery.

Two years earlier, in July 1999, I had reactivated discussions on this topic with the Regius Professor, Sir Keith Peters, as it became certain that Papworth would receive a lot of additional money to expand its cardiac surgical activity, so as to meet the exacting demands of the government's war on premature deaths and obscenely long waiting times for heart surgery.

My plan was to increase the number of consultant cardiac surgeons from seven to nine, although this initially met with some resistance from the surgeons, some of whom believed that a lot of their work would in future be undertaken by interventional cardiologists, so were fearful of being under-employed. There were also some other less charitable views, suggesting that the lucrative private patient market would diminish, and the surgeons wanted to protect their significant earnings from that source.

I persuaded the surgeons that expanding their numbers was essential, and reminded them of the impending European Working Time Directive, limiting working hours. Privately they had also told me that the increasing complexity of their work meant that the days when they could each carry out the 180–200 operations per year, and also be up all night doing transplant operations, were over.

In his response to my overture, Sir Keith Peters said that he "believed the university may be prepared to relax its policy on the private practice issue." This referred to the policy whereby Cambridge and, until recently, Oxford, would not allow their academic medical staff to undertake private practice.

Three months later, in October 1999, Sir Keith wrote to me again, saying that the university "had now made firm recommendations on arrangements for private practice, and I hope that these will create a climate in which we would be able to attract an outstanding Professor of Cardiac Surgery."

I kept my board informed of these exchanges, and Papworth's April board minutes recorded "the chief executive has been asked to put a case of need together with Professor Andrew Bradley (Professor of Surgery and Head of Department) for consideration at the next meeting of the university's general board. Because of the protracted process involved, the successful applicant was unlikely to be in post before October 2001."

My board agreed to support the appointment of both a professor and an assistant, called a 'university lecturer', on the understanding that funding would be provided via the national service framework (NSF) initiative, and, if necessary, charitable sources.

Andrew Bradley and I firmed up the details, which confirmed that the annual cost to Papworth would be circa £120,000. The amount of extra income that Papworth was due to receive from the NSF to fund our cardiac surgical expansion programme, amounted to over £2 million per annum over the next three years, as the government demanded that maximum waiting times came down to 13 weeks.

Stephen Donaldson's reply to the surgeons in February 2001 was clear. It read: "*Sir Keith was also very clear to me, when I spoke to him yesterday, that he expects the chair to be a practising surgeon [...] Whilst the timing may not be ideal, the risks in terms of operational issues are minimal. Again, this situation has not been helped by the delays in progressing our bid for new facilities, and if we had secured agreement to these when submitted back in July 2000, the theatre facility would be in place this summer.*"

Meanwhile, over at Bedford, I was getting telephone calls from Sir Keith and Alan Burns, both registering their concerns at the negative noises emanating from Papworth towards this initiative. They reminded me of my various assertions over the recent years that Papworth was serious about developing its academic potential, and how this was going to be a key feature of the very important Hinxton Hall conference, which was now only a few weeks away.

On 26th April 2001, my 25th anniversary of working for the NHS, I was invited to attend the official opening of Papworth's replacement Cardiac Unit, of 45 beds, the ceremony to be performed by National Director for Heart Disease, Professor Roger Boyle. This was also the day of the board meeting which, unusually, overran by one hour. When Audrey emerged, she looked very stressed, and seemed uncomfortable talking to me. I immediately put two and two together, and knew that there must have been a difficult discussion about the chair in cardiac surgery.

I did not have long to wait before having my suspicions confirmed. I received a copy of Audrey's letter to Sir Keith Peters, dated 3rd May. The board wanted to defer its final decision one month "in the hope that two areas of major concern could be resolved." Their first concern was "a perception that the process was not as open as it should have been", and requested that the post be advertised more widely. The second concern related to the funding of the chair: "Papworth simply does not have the money to finance in full [...] estimated at around £120,000, and it would be unthinkable to everyone concerned that an internal applicant should be made on the grounds of mere affordability."

Not surprisingly, this letter caused a furore at the clinical school, and it was not long before Regional Director, Peter Houghton, became involved. In a couple of telephone discussions I had had with Peter at Bedford, I had made him aware of my suspicions that Audrey may backtrack on this initiative. Peter had been involved in the early discussions on this topic, so he was well aware of the history. He now nailed his colours firmly to the mast, and wrote to Audrey Stenner on 23rd May. His letter read:

> *"As we discussed, this development is of great importance strategically, both to Papworth and the region. I have personally reinforced this in my discussions with Roger Boyle and other colleagues at the Department of Health. During your absence of leave, I met with Alan Burns and he is committed to ensuring that this development is funded. I expect the Papworth board to acknowledge this and play a positive role with Cambridgeshire Health Authority to achieve this. Secondly, I have met with Sir Keith Peters, and I am absolutely convinced of the integrity of the election process and confident that the university will ensure, as always, that the best possible candidate is appointed. I look*

forward to hearing a positive outcome from the Papworth Board meeting."

The stand-off over who should pay the £40,000 difference between Papworth's original offer, and my subsequent agreement with Professor Bradley, continued until the end of June, when Alan Burns confirmed, in writing, his Health Authority's pledge to meet this potential shortfall.

Audrey Stenner then wrote to Peter Houghton on 13th July, stating that Alan Burn's letter provided the Papworth board with the assurance it was seeking.

Also in July, the university took the decision to approach the British Heart Foundation (BHF) for funding for the professor's salary, and to consider an application for a personal professorship to complement the BHF-funded position.

This decision allayed any remaining concerns that were held by the Papworth board and some of the surgeons. On 20th June, Frank Wells, in his capacity as chairman of the Papworth Medical Advisory Committee, and a member of the appointments panel for this position, sent the following note to his consultant colleagues:

"An extensive international search is currently being undertaken to fill the chair in cardiac surgery. Many of you will know there has been an excellent response and that a number of

> *very highly regarded national and international cardiac surgeons have expressed an interest in this chair.*
>
> *On the basis of the exceptional quality of the field [...] the British Heart Foundation has indicated that they would be prepared to fund one post [...] If the application to the BHF is successful, the professorship of cardiac surgery will complement the chair in cardiothoracic surgery in a similar way to the two chairs in the academic Department of Respiratory Medicine, which have been highly successful and enabled Cambridge to achieve a centre of excellence that others now aspire to.*
>
> *The opportunity for a chair in cardiac surgery is a truly exciting development and one that we should not let slip from our grasp."*

Eventually, in 2002, an American cardiac surgeon – BR – who had worked at Papworth some years before in a junior capacity on the transplant programme, was appointed as the BHF chair for cardiac surgery.

John Wallwork, Papworth's medical director, internationally acclaimed cardiothoracic surgeon, and pioneer in heart and lung transplantation, was awarded a personal chair by the University of Cambridge.

It is fair to say that the expectations for the academic department of cardiac surgery were not fulfilled, and BR returned to the USA in 2007.

We decided not to seek a successor as several other academic centres in the UK had failed to appoint to their vacancies.

Meanwhile, in April 2001, a very successful conference was held at Hinxton Hall, with 114 delegates attending, mainly from Papworth and Addenbrooke's, and colleagues from Cambridgeshire Health Authority, the regional office, and University of Cambridge. The clinicians worked well together over the two days and fashioned a clinical vision for cardiothoracic services for the east of England, covering the next 10–15 years.

I took the various drafts from the working groups, and together with a lot of help from colleagues, produced a clinical vision document, which we believed would provide the evidence to underpin the business case for a new Papworth Hospital on land adjacent to Addenbrooke's Hospital.

In May 2001, the regional office set up a working party to assess whether a second cardiothoracic centre was needed for the east of England. This was due to the persistent lobbying of Malcolm Stamp, CEO, at the Norfolk and Norwich Hospital, who already undertook thoracic surgery, and understandably hoped that they could set up cardiac surgery now that the NSF for heart disease had been published by the government.

The chair of the regional working party was Andrew Reed, the CEO of the soon-to-be abolished Bedfordshire Health Authority and, from September 2001, my successor as CEO at Bedford Hospital.

Replacing the roof on my house

On the evening of Andrew's interview for the Bedford Hospital post, 27th June, my house suffered a severe lightning strike, and was minutes away from catching fire, but was saved by the volunteer firemen from Papworth, who included several hospital staff. I realised that it was 12 months to the day since my wallet had been stolen: 27th June was obviously not a good day in the Bridge household!

I went to work as normal the next day, not yet aware of the severity of the damage to my house, and told the Bedford Hospital. Chairman Andy Blowers felt that it would be best if I handed over to Andrew Reed sooner rather than later.

As I had accrued several weeks of annual leave – circumstances at Bedford had prevented me from taking a break – and with Andrew's close proximity, I asked if I could take some time off, and return to Papworth.

As swiftly as I joined Bedford back in mid-January, I now departed as rapidly, saying my farewells to lot of decent people who worked exceptionally hard to restore the hospital's tarnished reputation. I even got a pleasant send off from *The Beds on Sunday* newspaper, the one which broke the mortuary story and sold it to the national media. Having heard of the severe damage to my house they ran a headline: 'Chief Makes Lightning Exit and Leaves the Sinking Ship.'

A couple of months later I received a pleasant letter from the new chair at Bedford Hospital, Helen Nellis:

26-JUL-2001 14:52 FROM TO 901480831315 P.02

Leaderless again: Lightning departure for temporary chief

Bridge abandons troubled hospital

BEDFORD Hospital's acting chief executive has quit in a hurry after his house was struck by lightning.

Stephen Bridge, who is the top man at Papworth Hospital, Cambridge, took over as temporary boss at Bedford Hospital when former chief executive Ken Williams stood down following the bodies in the chapel scandal exposed by *Bedfordshire on Sunday* earlier this year.

The post of chief executive was widely advertised but in May the hospital called off interviews at short notice amid rumours, strenuously denied, that candidates had pulled out when they heard Bedford was to be downgraded to non-emergency services only in the Government's health review.

At the beginning of July, Andrew Reed, chief executive of Bedfordshire Health Authority, was appointed Bedford Hospital's new chief executive but he does not take up the post full-time until September and Mr Bridge was expected to stay until his arrival.

But at the end of last week, Mr Bridge suddenly went back to Papworth, leaving Bedford once again leaderless and prompting criticism from a senior doctor.

Mr Bridge said: "I had intended to stay longer but holiday commitments and a number of personal issues, not least that my house has been struck by lightning, meant I would only be there on a very part time basis. I had a meeting with the chairman and it was decided that I could be released."

However, Dr Richard Rawlins, consultant orthopaedic surgeon, said: "It never rains but it pours. We have had our problems this year and it is a shame that Mr Bridge has felt it necessary to leave before his replacement is in place because he was doing a good job."

"I know that his house has been struck by lightning, which seems like a fairly reasonable explanation, but I understand he is back at work at Papworth and if he can work at Papworth why not at Bedford?"

■ Lightning exit: Stephen Bridge, who has returned to Papworth after a short stay at Bedford Hospital following the Bodies in the Chapel scandal

'I understand he is back at work at Papworth and if he can work at Papworth why not at Bedford?'

– Consultant surgeon Dr Richard Rawlins

> *"Dear Stephen,*
>
> *I wanted to write to thank you for the excellent job that you have done at Bedford Hospital. You came at a most difficult time and managed to earn the respect and confidence of colleagues who were feeling rather bruised and demoralised by events. You were successful not only in stabilising the situation, but also in setting the hospital off in a new direction."*

A further letter from Peter Houghton, the regional director, said:

> *"It is a clear measure of how well you have done that so many people have expressed to me their regret that they could not persuade you to apply for the job on a permanent basis."*

As soon as I returned to Papworth I became fully engaged with the region-wide exercise to decide whether a second cardiothoracic centre was needed.

After a very thorough exercise, the recommendation was that a second cardiothoracic centre for the eastern region was necessary, but should be located in Essex or Hertfordshire. After a further piece of work, Basildon pipped Chelmsford to host the new centre. In one of those bizarre pieces of timing that the NHS seems to thrive on, the announcement of the Basildon centre was made at about the same time as Bart's Hospital was allowed to sign off the biggest PFI scheme in health, despite the knowledge that it would lose millions of pounds of income from cardiac referrals to the new centre at Basildon

This eventful year drew to a close with the government removing the greenbelt status of the land adjacent to Addenbrooke's, and a new chairman being appointed to Papworth.

Audrey Stenner had served three terms of four, three and two years respectively, and had expected to get one final year. However, her uncompromising stance on the move to Cambridge, and her difficult relationship with the regional office, recently illustrated by her position on the chair in cardiac surgery, led them to conclude that it was time for a change.

The regional office informed Audrey in September that she would not be getting a new term, and Peter Houghton rang to tell me that a businessman would be our new chair.

On 1st November, John Beadsmoore joined us, having retired after a long career with Ciba Geigy, the international pharmaceuticals company. John had made his views clear in his pre-interview visits that he was not impressed with the calibre of NHS management.

Out of the frying pan into the fire, was one thought that came into my head.

CHAPTER FOURTEEN

2002-03

"Volunteer for Everything"

John Beadsmoore's view of NHS management's shortcomings was reinforced after attending his first meeting of the Cambridge Health Authority-led steering group, chaired by its CEO, Alan Burns. This group was responsible for the planned reconfiguration of acute and community services across the county. Following that meeting, John suggested that he and I should get to work and write the strategic outline case (SOC) for the move of Papworth to Cambridge, and not leave it to the 'talking shop' of local NHS groups.

We duly got down to work, and by early January 2002 he and I had finished the document, and, in the process, forged a good bond between us. Following strong support from our purchasing Health Authorities, we submitted our SOC to the regional office, who promised to forward it to the Department of Health. In late February we were informed by the regional office that DH had said that their new policy was to wait until they issued a national call for major capital projects; in other words, 'don't call us, we'll call you'.

The remainder of 2002 was dominated by the implementation of the NHS Plan, the government's blueprint for major investment and reform, including the allocation of significant extra money for cancer and heart disease, and the overhaul of terms and conditions of all staff. I was pleased to see Papworth first on the list of world-class hospitals mentioned in the Plan, and hoped this augured well for future discussions about our new hospital in Cambridge.

The negotiations surrounding a new contract for consultant medical staff got bogged down – and the national press, particularly *The Times* newspaper, took exception to this, and ran several articles under the heading 'Blair Initiative Runs Aground on Rock of Medical Establishment'. This referred to a government plan to recruit foreign consultants called the 'International Fellowship Scheme', to bridge the gap until the additional doctors promised in the NHS Plan finished their training. The prime minister had appointed Professor Sir Magdi Yacoub, the renowned cardiac and transplant surgeon from the Royal Brompton and Harefield hospitals, as his special ambassador to lead on this initiative. For some strange reason, Professor Yacoub chose cardiac surgery as one of the specialties in the first wave of this initiative, even though there was no shortage of doctors at senior registrar level in the UK hoping soon be appointed to a consultant post.

As the arguments raged between the Department of Health and the British Medical Association, the permanent secretary of the Department of Health and the NHS, CEO Nigel Crisp summoned the CEOs of the ten biggest cardiac centres to a meeting in Birmingham to discuss the International Fellowship Scheme. At this meeting we had to show evidence of our cardiac surgical productivity: Papworth was both the biggest centre and the most efficient, with each of our surgeons carrying out an average of 180 operations per year. As such, I assumed that I would not be one of the CEOs who would be invited to 'accept an offer that they could not refuse'.

However, I was wrong, and a few days later I received a telephone call from Peter Houghton telling me there was heavy pressure from Number 10 to show that this IFS initiative was successful and, as Papworth was a flagship cardiac hospital, we were expected to sign up.

The more Peter explained the details of the initiative the less I liked it. Participating centres would also be expected to meet the salary costs for the two or three years' duration, and no guarantee was given that the costs of the extra operations carried out by the 'International Fellow' would be paid by our purchasers.

Papworth had only just increased its consultant cardiac surgical workforce from seven to nine, and the rumblings around the chair in cardiac surgery had not yet fully subsided, so it was going to be a very tall order for me to persuade our consultants that we needed another surgeon.

More telephone calls came from regional office, including one from Paul Kemp, who, as ever, understood my predicament, and said he would enquire if there was any leeway regarding participating centres having to meet the salary costs. A few days later I got a call from Avril Johns, formerly CEO at Chesterfield Hospital, and recently seconded to David Nicholson's team, Nigel Crisp's supremo in performance management, or 'enforcer' as he was becoming known in senior management circles!

Avril asked me to let her have the annual costs I anticipated resulting from this initiative, and she would 'take it up the line'. My finance director, Stephen Donaldson, and I agreed that £600,000 per annum was a fair figure, so we sent this information to Avril without further delay.

Before I had a response from Avril Johns, another problem arose.

I was driving back from Lancaster University, having completed the third module of the NHS Senior Leaders Programme – a mandatory programme to ensure that NHS CEOs were up for the challenge of implementing the NHS Plan – and as I neared Peterborough, I got an urgent call from Avril. Apparently Frank Wells, my colleague and British Medical Association local representative, had contacted David Nicholson's office and told them in no uncertain terms that the International Fellowship Scheme was not needed, and it was jeopardising the career prospects of the 33 UK senior registrars who had finished their training and were waiting to be appointed as consultants.

I expected a bollocking, but instead Avril asked me if I could ask Frank to back off. As I did not want to jeopardise the prospect of Papworth obtaining the £1.2 million we had asked for the two-year duration of this scheme, I rang my secretary, Barbara, and asked her to get Frank to come to my office in one hour. Upon receiving this message, Frank assumed that he was in hot water, so telephoned the president of the Royal College of Surgeons, Sir Peter Morris.

Just after I returned to my office, Sir Peter telephoned me – we had met when I was doing the Oxford review in 2000, where he was a highly respected renal surgeon – and told me that Frank had called him and thought that I might suspend him, given the highly politically charged atmosphere surrounding the IFS. I told Sir Peter that nothing of the sort was going to happen, but would he mind not telling Frank that, as I wanted to keep Frank stewing, and exact a mild form of retribution on him for the couple of times he had got me into hot water with my superiors since I started at Papworth.

Sir Peter agreed to play along.

When Frank Wells entered my office, he did not know what to expect. I kept the joke going for a few minutes, but then told him that he needed to trust me, and support my plan to get some serious money for Papworth. I also said that I thought this International Fellowship Scheme would be quietly kicked into the long grass after a couple of symbolic appointments had been made. Hence, there would be no threat to the 33 UK doctors hoping to be appointed as consultant cardiothoracic surgeons. Frank saw the funny side of my ruse with Sir Peter, and said he trusted my judgement and would refrain from anymore chastising of the Department of Health, and wished me luck in my pursuit of a sizeable chunk of money to enable us to treat even more patients.

Within two days this amount was agreed, and I subsequently attended an interview panel in London where Guy's and St Thomas, Papworth, and Stoke hospitals selected three European candidates. We appointed a doctor from the Czech Republic, whose English was poor, so he spent an enjoyable two years at Papworth assisting our consultants and honing his skills in heart and lung transplants, such that he was able to set up a programme when he returned home.

When I was first introduced by Malcolm Stamp to David Nicholson a couple of years later, David greeted me with the phrase "Hello, moneybags," his renowned sense of humour seeing the funny side of a somewhat surreal exercise of a couple of years previously.

The final months of 2002 saw the culmination of two exciting projects which my director of research and development, Noreen Caine, had initiated. The first was the creation of an organisation that would help NHS inventions to get to the private market and achieve commercial returns. This organisation became known as Health Enterprise East, and was based at Papworth and initially managed by us until 2007, when we transferred it to the Strategic Health Authority.

The second of Noreen's great ideas was a research incubator, a building which would house small start-up companies working in the cardiothoracic field, which would then move on to bigger and better things, at which time Papworth and the wider NHS would receive a share of income via intellectual property rights agreements. We managed to secure £1.45 million in capital funds from the Regional Development Agency to provide a new building at Papworth.

Despite John Beadsmoore's initial support for these two initiatives, he suddenly became vehemently opposed to them, saying that I had exceeded my authority, and was leaving the board exposed to financial risk. After several tense board discussions, John Wallwork and I were able to persuade our non-executives that extensive due diligence had been undertaken, and these two initiatives were totally in keeping with Papworth's pioneering tradition of taking calculated risks.

Health Enterprise East is still going strong in 2019, cited by the Department of Health as the 'leading organisation of its type in the NHS', and the Research Incubator Building, a very posh 'temporary-type' facility, provided valuable space for an ever expanding Papworth right through to the move to Cambridge in 2019.

The beginning of 2003 saw the government unveiling its plans for top performing hospitals to become foundation trusts, directly accountable to Parliament.

Once again, my chairman John Beadsmoore and I joined forces and wrote our application document. We were delighted to hear in May that Papworth had been selected as one of the 29 hospitals approved by Secretary of State, Alan Milburn, to go forward and apply for first-wave FT status.

To be eligible for FT status, the hospital had to have been awarded the top mark of three stars by the Commission for Healthcare Improvement in its annual ratings exercise. For acute and specialist hospitals, this also meant having no patients waiting longer than 13 weeks for cardiac surgery at the end of March 2003. As the largest cardiac surgical centre in the country, Papworth also had the biggest waiting list, with more than 100 patients waiting over 13 weeks, as at the summer of 2002.

In all of the 30 NHS hospitals that carried out cardiac surgery in England, managers were negotiating extra payments with their surgeons, euphemistically called 'waiting list initiative', and Papworth was no exception. To achieve a position where nobody waited more than 13 weeks would entail a lot of additional operations being carried out in the evenings and weekends, whilst at the same time ensuring that other emergency operations, such as transplants, were also carried out.

After some hard bargaining, I agreed a deal with the surgeons, which although less expensive than the rates agreed in other hospitals, was still mouth-wateringly high because of the volume of extra operations we needed to carry out.

Understandably, my chairman was concerned at the large sums of money that we would be paying out to the eight surgeons, 12 anaesthetists, and the overtime payments to the dozens of other staff working in the operating theatres. The board resolved to award all staff a £250 bonus, should we achieve the 13-week maximum waiting time target by March 2003.

As John Beadsmoore wrote in his letter to the surgeons on 26th July: "*You should be aware that this payment has caused the board much anguish! So, the purpose of this note is to tell you that Stephen Bridge has worked very hard on your behalf, so please do not let us down and not perform the demanding number of operations we have agreed for the current year.*"

The Foundation Trust Bill was fiercely debated in the House of Commons, with the government securing only a narrow win when the first reading took place in September. The Bill was then defeated in the House of Lords, and just scraped through on its third reading in the House of Commons on 18th November. It was said that Prime Minister Blair was prepared to resign had the government lost the vote, as he regarded the foundation trust initiative as a cornerstone of his policy to reform the English healthcare system.

In late spring, the CEO of Addenbrooke's, Roy Male, asked to meet me one evening for a pint, as he wanted to discuss matters of a personal nature. I liked and respected Roy, particularly as he had given me invaluable advice when he was the director of human resources at

Addenbrooke's on a delicate issue I was facing at Papworth in early 1993. Ten years later Roy was looking to exit one of the plum jobs in the NHS. He told me there were two reasons: family ties in Lancashire, and the opportunity to set up a new cardiac centre at Blackpool Hospital. He also told me of the impending announcement that Mary Archer was to be the next chairman of Addenbrooke's and said that now was a good time for him to seek pastures new.

A few months later the Addenbrooke's board, now chaired by Lady Mary Archer, opted to change its name to Cambridge University Hospitals NHS Trust. This unnerved my chairman and the non-executives, feeling that it was a precursor to them formally proposing that Papworth should withdraw our FT application and merge with, or more accurately, be taken over, by this large teaching hospital. I was much more sanguine, having 'sparred' with my large neighbour several times during the 15 years I had been at Papworth, and advised my board to keep our eye on the ball, i.e. maintain an efficient hospital, and this would ensure that we became a foundation trust in our own right.

One of the reasons why I was unperturbed was the view held by a previous chairman of Addenbrooke's, Sir John Bradfield. On the one or two occasions I met him each year, after he stepped down as chairman of Addenbrooke's in 1997, he would ask me how our move to Cambridge was progressing. Then he would say, "Dear boy, I am pleased to hear things are moving forward, but whatever you do, do not lose your identity." Those words, coming from such a hugely respected and successful person, stayed with me all through the various threats to Papworth's independence which we were to face over the coming years.

At two successive national meetings for aspirant foundation trusts, Mary Archer asked Nigel Crisp, and John Reid, the new secretary of state, if they supported the concept of a 'community of FTs', proposing that smaller trusts should withdraw their applications, and throw their lot in with their larger neighbours.

As a mild act of retaliation, and with my tongue firmly in my cheek, during one of the public consultation meetings Papworth held to discuss our bid for FT status, at which Mary Archer was in the audience, I gave an undertaking that, following Papworth's hoped-for move to the Cambridge Biomedical Campus, Papworth "would not seek to take over Addenbrooke's for at least five years." Needless to say, Mary was not amused.

Undeterred, Mary Archer had persuaded the chair of the Huntingdon(shire) primary care trust, Michael Lynch, a key commissioner of Papworth's services, to propose a motion at his board meeting that Papworth should withdraw its FT application, and submit a joint application with Addenbrooke's/Cambridge University Hospitals. At the meeting – which I had decided not to attend, instead opting to go to a consultation meeting in a Peterborough pub, which was then overrun with Manchester United supporters on their way to a pre-season football match – I was later told by our representative at the PCT meeting, Ken Brewer, of the moment of high drama.

Michael Lynch had not bothered to tell his CEO, Karen Bell, of his plan. Karen – a colleague I had known for several years and had hoped to appoint as my director of human resources in 1993 – was fully supportive of Papworth retaining its separate identity. Karen boldly spoke against the motion, and won the vote on a show of hands, and our bid for FT status was duly supported. Had the vote gone the other way, it could have meant the end of our application, as this primary care trust was our largest commissioner, and its vote of no confidence in our bid to be a first-wave foundation trust would, I have no doubt, resulted in Papworth being told by the Department of Health to merge, or more accurately, be taken over by Cambridge University Hospitals.

If that had happened, Papworth would now be sandwiched into three floors of Addenbrooke's Hospital, instead of celebrating the opening of a state-of-the-art, standalone building, the envy of the NHS.

There was one more surprise in store in 2003, and that was the appointment of Malcolm Stamp as CEO of Cambridge University Hospitals in December. Malcolm was quick off the mark, and on only his third day in his new role, he requested that I attend an urgent meeting with Peter Houghton and himself. At this meeting I was pressed by Malcolm to give dates for certain milestones for our move to Cambridge, and left in no doubt that the clock was ticking, and if Papworth failed to make significant progress in the next few months, then he reserved the right to establish a rival cardiology service at CUH.

CHAPTER FIFTEEN

2004-05

Cambridge: The Journey Begins

I was relieved, therefore, when in January 2004 the Department of Health issued invitations for the submission of major capital projects, initially with a strategic outline case to be sent to them by the end of March. They stressed that only a few would be successful, but in the event, all 15 SOCs submitted were approved in July to proceed to the next stage, the outline business case (OBC). Hitherto, the OBC stage usually took around 12–18 months, but little did I know that we were about to enter an era of constant change, with six secretaries of state for health coming and going over the next 11 years, each with their own views on how the private finance initiative approach should be handled.

On 1st July 2004, both Papworth and Cambridge University Hospitals were granted foundation trust status, two of the first 20. My board naturally believed the government line, and expected a light-touch regulation

regime to follow, especially the fast-track processing of our OBC. Neither of these hopes materialised, with Monitor, the new regulator for foundation trusts, taking an interventionist approach right from its inception, led by their executive chairman, William (Bill) Moyes. This was not the light-touch approach that had been promised, but now that that Alan Milburn had departed the scene, and the prime minister's focus had now moved away from the NHS, several senior NHS figures, including David Nicholson, saw this as an opportunity to reassert the authority of the 'centre'.

The new FTs needed an effective organisation to represent their views. I was invited to a meeting at the Reform Club, Pall Mall, London, convened by Mark Britnell, the charismatic CEO of University of Birmingham Hospitals, someone who had the ear of Sir Nigel Crisp, the NHS CEO.

This meeting was also attended by other aspirant foundation trust CEOs, Robert Naylor, Malcolm Stamp, Malcolm Lowe-Lauri and Ian Balmer from University College London, Cambridge University Hospitals, King's College Hospital, and Moorfields. Mark told us that the NHS establishment would not be happy if the first-wave FTs pursued their new freedoms with vigour; instead they wanted a low-key lobbying group to represent FTs. We were urged not to repeat the mistake of the early 1990s when the equivalent trust federation was seen to be too right wing and too forthright, and failed to gain ministerial access. As a result, it was taken over by the centrist/left-

leaning National Association of Health Authorities and Trusts to become the NHS Confederation.

Mark's advice was not accepted by the more hawkish members among us, so he gracefully stepped aside and allowed Malcolm Lowe-Lauri to take matters forward. The Foundation Trust Network was duly set up, consisting of the 20 first-wave FTs, but as Mark Britnell had so rightly predicted, it eventually rebranded itself as NHS Providers and pursued a less confrontational line in order to gain greater access to ministers.

Production of Papworth's OBC continued into 2005, co-ordinated by our very able project director, Ken Brewer, whom I had appointed in 2001 initially to update our strategic plan, later becoming project manager for our foundation trust application. I had no hesitation in entrusting the project leadership of the new hospital to Ken, and he soon became an expert on the complex European Union rules governing the PFI process.

The public consultation phase took place in the summer of 2005, and I was delighted in September when a specially convened Overview and Scrutiny Committee, comprising all OSCs from across eastern England, chaired by Cambridgeshire County Council, voted 8–0 in favour of our proposed move to Cambridge. These committees had statutory powers in major reconfigurations, and a vote against the move would have had dire consequences for the project.

However…

Two major adverse events occurred in 2005 which could have blown our OBC off course had we mishandled them.

The first of these occurred during the summer, when John Beadsmoore, our chairman, felt that we needed an updated and unequivocal board minute stating our wish to move to the Cambridge Biomedical Campus. Delving back into our archives, I produced an audit trail of the many detailed discussions, and John and I fashioned a clearer resolution, subsequently approved by the board, in support of the move to the CBC. Armed with this updated mandate, John B requested a meeting of our counterparts, Mary Archer and Malcolm Stamp from Cambridge University Hospitals, and Stewart Francis and Peter Houghton, from the Strategic Health Authority. At this meeting John went to great lengths to explain how, when appointed, he was urged by the then SHA chairman, Rosie Varley, to speed up the move of Papworth to Cambridge. He was particularly concerned about keeping the support of the sceptical Papworth board of governors, who, despite having limited powers, had the 'nuclear option' and could fire the chairman and put a spanner in the works with regard to strategic change, i.e. the move to Cambridge.

Mary Archer felt that the minute did not go far enough, as I felt she wanted to prise the door open for a merger between our two hospitals. There were several sharp exchanges between her and John Beadsmoore, culminating in John saying that he had gone out on a

limb and could not persuade the board or the governors to go any further at this current time. In an astonishing retort, Mary Archer said, "Frankly, I don't believe you."

John's reply was that those words were the most insulting he had received in 37 years of professional life, and the meeting ended with the three chairmen leaving the room.

Fortunately, this uncomfortable spat did not affect the working relationship between Malcolm and me, both of us having many years' experience in working with strong characters.

The second adverse event took place at the end of September. At the end of our board meeting, and without any discussion with me beforehand, John Beadsmoore announced that he would not seek a second term, and he would stand down at the end of October. After some discussion, he agreed that he would stay on until Christmas, to give us more time to find a successor. His robust style had resulted in him receiving feedback in the 360-degree appraisal which he could not accept – hence he felt the only way out was to resign. Back in his office I asked him if he had any more surprises up his sleeve, to which he replied that he had lost the confidence of the non-executives, so felt that he had no alternative but to resign.

Whilst John's departure would have no effect on the operational running of the hospital, I was acutely aware of the political ramifications it might have with Monitor, the Strategic Health Authority, and the Department of

Health, with regard to their support for our business case for the move to Cambridge.

At the end of our October board meeting, John gave a short speech and said he would leave in four days, and his final comment was that the only way forward for Papworth was to merge with Cambridge University Hospitals. I decided not to challenge him, as he looked very tired. Instead, as it was my 50th birthday in a couple of days and we were planning a family weekend away, I suggested I cut it short by a day so that we could go for lunch on the Monday. When Monday came, I popped into work at lunchtime, only to be told that he had come in early, packed his things, dictated several critical letters, including one to Bill Moyes, and left the building. I couldn't help thinking that 10 years to the day, since receiving the go-ahead for our first business case (to redevelop at Papworth), on another milestone birthday for me, the curse of the project had struck again and our outgoing chairman had let it be known to several influential people that a merger with Cambridge University Hospitals was the right course of action to take.

CHAPTER SIXTEEN

2006-07

Addenbrooke's Sneezes, so Papworth Catches a Cold

The search for a new chairman went smoothly, with the non-executive directors, led by Professor Michael Simmonds, and senior governors, led by their senior, Air Vice Marshall John Brownlow, entrusting me with managing the process, and informing them of progress at least twice a week. My visits to John's house were particularly enjoyable, as it coincided with that great British tradition of many people of his generation: a 'sundowner' of a good size gin and tonic.

The interview took place in February 2006, with a panel comprising senior governors, non-executives and a chairman from another specialist foundation trust as outside assessor. The successful candidate was Robert Burgin who, until four years previously, was CEO of the Cambridge Water Company and now held non-executive roles on two other public sector boards, the

Armed Services Pay Review Body, and a large housing association.

Cambridge is a relatively small place, so as soon as news spread of Robert's appointment I received a couple of phone calls from his previous associates. I was told that he was very nice, but could 'talk for England', a fault that I too suffer from. It had been known, they continued, for colleagues to turn the lights off and leave the room, as a non-too subtle hint that it was late and they had homes to go to.

My first meeting with Robert, following his appointment, was on a Friday afternoon, and we had arranged a tour of the hospital for him. This took longer than expected, since being an engineer, he was fascinated by the hospital's ageing infrastructure, and spent a fair amount of time examining the boilers.

Arriving in my office at 6pm, we were still talking at 9pm. Given my experience with my previous two chairs, i.e. their propensity to become executive, I decided to 'go for it' and put a marker down with my new chairman: I told him there was more than enough work to do to keep us both gainfully employed, but I did not want him to stray into my territory.

Robert came to see me the following Monday and, to his great credit, he told me that the temptation for him to interfere in operational matters would be too great if his office was next to mine, as had been the case for the past 13 years. He therefore proposed that he should move to Papworth Hall, the grade II listed building we rented from the other Papworth trust.

There began a harmonious working relationship lasting for the next nine years.

Over a six-week period, from April to mid-May, Papworth became embroiled in what the media christened 'health tourism'. As one of only six adult heart and lung transplant centres in the UK, we were used to receiving patients from many hospitals. We had developed effective clinical protocols to ensure that only appropriate patients were admitted to Papworth, and the increasing number of non-clinical rules emanating from the Department of Health were always followed.

This case involved a 28-year-old Nigerian lady who, on a visit to the UK, gave birth to twins in Basildon Hospital. After she was discharged, she developed heart failure and was admitted to the Queen Elizabeth Hospital, Woolwich, southeast London. They referred her to Papworth, and it soon became apparent that she would need a heart transplant, and this lady's partner went to court to try and get her placed on the waiting list for an urgent transplant. The judge adjourned the hearing, and referred the matter to the Home Office to determine her immigration status.

Papworth's legal advisers were the company Mills & Reeve, whose Cambridge office had taken over the in-house NHS legal team serving East Anglia in the run up to the Thatcher reforms in 1991. Papworth had retained Mills & Reeves following several competitive tendering exercises, and their knowledge of the NHS was extensive. Their head of health practice, David Lock, was a barrister based in their Birmingham office, but prior to that he had been the MP for Wyre Forest, and lost his seat to my former Kidderminster Hospital colleague, Dr Richard Taylor, a victory that sent shockwaves across the political scene, and which, to this day, makes MPs with small majorities think long and hard before supporting controversial changes to the NHS in their constituencies.

During the time that the Home Office were considering the case, the lady died. The media covered the story extensively, as it was one of the first cases involving the jurisdiction of the European Court of Human Rights, with *The Daily Mail* and *The Independent* newspapers not surprisingly taking opposite views in this complex case with their front page stories.

Across our Strategic Health Authority both performance and the financial position were bleak and had been for some time. The chairman, CEO, and director of finance (Stewart Francis, Peter Houghton and Paul Kemp) all paid the price, and were removed from office.

A few weeks before this coup d'état, our regional meeting of CEOs was addressed by David Nicholson and his team from the top performing Midlands region. They were about to be sent in by Nigel Crisp, to try and find the reasons for the major problems in our patch. David Nicholson pulled no punches in his dressing down of the assembled CEOs, and whilst we were having a coffee break I pointed out to my fellow CEO from King's Lynn Hospital, Richard Venning, that there was a chauffeur-driven, top-of-the-range Mercedes S Class limousine outside the building, ready to whisk David Nicholson away. I had to admire this piece of showmanship, as if the tough man from the north was telling us soft southerners, "Look what your reward can be if you deliver on your bottom line."

A new leadership team was put in place at the SHA. Keith Pearson, a non-executive director at Peterborough and Stamford Hospital, became the new chairman, and Alan Burns and Steve Clarke, formerly of this patch, now CEO/director of finance respectively in the adjacent Trent SHA, were parachuted in. Paul Kemp took early retirement, and I organised a dinner for him in recognition of his sterling work over the past 15 years, particularly his bravery in helping me secure capital investment at Papworth during my early days at the hospital.

After Alan Burns' sudden departure from the scene a few months later, two caretaker CEOs followed in quick succession, whilst the search continued for a strong leader with a track record to be the new permanent CEO of this troubled part of the NHS.

Changes in leadership also occurred at Cambridge University Hospitals, with Malcolm Stamp's brief tenure ending with his shock departure for New Zealand. When I asked Malcolm the reasons for his move, he replied that he felt like a change; but one thing was for sure: if he ever returned to work in the NHS, it would not be in London or at regional level.

Six months later, as I was waiting to go through security at Portcullis House, Westminster, to have lunch with the MP for Kidderminster and ex-colleague, Dr Richard Taylor, my phone rang. It was a headhunting firm, asking me if I was interested in Malcolm's post in New Zealand, as their client had 'accepted a job of a lifetime' heading up the provider office of the London Strategic Health Authority!

The new CEO at CUH, Gareth Goodier, started in September 2006. I had first met Gareth several years earlier when he was appointed CEO at the Royal Brompton and Harefield trust. Gareth then moved to become the CEO of the SHA in northwest London, and became caught up in the infamous, i.e. aborted PFI scheme at Paddington Basin, involving St Mary's Hospital and the Royal Brompton and Harefield Hospitals.

At our first meeting he asked me to suspend the roll out of the new heart attack service at Papworth, and instead set it up in his hospital. He also said he wanted Papworth to take over the running of the small cardiology service at Addenbrooke's, set up by Malcolm Stamp a few years earlier. Much as I liked Gareth, there was no certainty that he could find the money or space to implement his idea, let alone bring his senior medical staff on board. On the other hand, Papworth was due to implement the new 24/7 heart attack service in a matter of weeks, as we had led on this SHA-brokered initiative, overseen by their medical director, Robert Winter (formerly medical director and acting CEO at Cambridge University Hospitals).

This very important, complex and often controversial initiative was driven forward with great skill and determination by two senior Papworth clinicians, Dr Sarah Clarke, an interventional cardiologist, and Ann-Marie Ingle, a senior nurse. I explained to Gareth that to make a change at this very late stage would also potentially undermine our business case, only recently reprieved, and that we could achieve a win-win by exploring other areas of collaboration in cardiology, and working together to achieve the speedy relocation of Papworth to the extended Cambridge Biomedical Campus.

In December 2006, the SHA appointed a permanent CEO, Neil McKay, one of the big hitters in NHS management with an impressive CV, including being CEO of Sheffield and Leeds teaching hospitals, and a spell as chief operating officer at the Department of Health. Although I did not know Neil McKay well, I suspected that his time at Sheffield and Leeds would have given him a good understanding of cardiothoracic services, and why they needed to be part of the teaching hospital / academic environment. I managed to get an appointment to see him on the Friday afternoon of his first week at our SHA. The venue was a hotel in Grantham, just off the A1, as he returned home to Doncaster, and me, heading south, after my one and only visit to the 'Kremlin', aka Quarry House, Leeds, the main Department of Health office in northern England.

I was naturally keen to know if he would help to make our move to Cambridge a reality, especially in light of yet another Treasury-initiated review of NHS PFI schemes. Neil gave nothing away, but was generally encouraging.

Our conversation then turned to the appointment of a new CEO for Peterborough Hospital, where I was to be outside assessor, one of the candidates being Neil's deputy at Leeds, Nick Patten.

Just before the year-end, on 20th and 21st December, we had a two-day visit from the Department of Health team reviewing the PFI schemes. They were experienced project managers of earlier PFI projects, seconded to the department, who left no stone unturned in their pursuit of testing the robustness of all aspects of the project, including the strength of support from our key purchasers/commissioners and stakeholders, and the expertise of our project team. With the rapid turnover of senior staff in our main primary care trusts, I spent a lot of time contacting the new incumbents and trying to shore up their previous support, against a backdrop of the worsening financial position across the SHA.

Maintaining the SHA's strategic support was, as previously mentioned, crucial. My principal point of contact for this was Dr Paul Watson, their director of commissioning. I had first met Paul in 1994, when, as an up-and-coming force in the public health department of the Cambridge and Huntingdon Health Authority, he used to harangue me for not moving faster with the move of Papworth to Addenbrooke's. I was hoping that he would channel his enthusiasm for the move into cajoling the PCTs to provide me with strong letters of support for the projected patient activity increases, and their financial implications that underpinned our business case for the move.

In the first three months of 2007, I managed to secure the support of all the primary care trusts in our catchment area, which, along with the support of the National Specialised Services Commissioning Group, constituted over 80% of Papworth's income, the threshold necessary if the scheme was to survive. This evidence was given to the review team, upon their second-stage visit on 4th April 2007.Their team leader, Richard Glenn, seemed satisfied with the hard evidence, but his parting words to me in private left me with an uneasy feeling. He advised me to change the project team, saying he did not feel they were tough enough to withstand the rigours of the next stage, especially dealing with the savvy and tough negotiators from the private sector PFI firms and their advisers.

After a nail-biting wait of two months, during which time I had resolved to stick with the current project team, I received a letter from the Department of Health on 14th June, giving Papworth the go-ahead to proceed to the outline business case stage.

The letter stated:

> *"The OBC will need to demonstrate that the issues of co-location have been adequately dealt with, and in particular that the lessons of the Paddington project have been addressed. To this end it is recommended that a joint briefing*

and scoping team, with membership from both organisations is established as soon as possible to aid in the development of the project."

This referred to the Parliamentary, i.e. Public Accounts Committee Enquiry, into the Paddington Basin fiasco, when the scheme was aborted, partly due to our 'sister' hospital, the Royal Brompton and Harefield's refusal to merge with its PFI partner, St Mary's Hospital. Several million pounds of fees were consequently written off.

Parliament thus stated that if two NHS trusts came together to sponsor a PFI scheme, then they should merge in order to increase the chance of success for the project. As Papworth was planning to purchase land on that segment of the Cambridge Biomedical Campus which was owned by the private developers, having been 'evicted' from the cheaper NHS-designated land some years earlier by Malcolm Stamp, then we were fully compliant with this Parliamentary requirement.

The capital limit was £124.6 million, and the unitary payment, i.e. the mortgage, was not to exceed £15.48 million. "*If any of these conditions are breached, the scheme will require a complete re-appraisal process*," the letter concluded.

As Gareth Goodier had been the CEO of the northwest London SHA overseeing the Paddington Basin scheme, and who had been 'put through the mill' by the Public Accounts Committee, I hoped that he would now throw his weight behind our PFI scheme, and atone for his past mistakes in London.

As several other schemes had failed this Departmental of Health review, I was naturally pleased and relieved that Papworth's scheme was to be allowed to continue.

However, this euphoria lasted little more than one month.

On 25th July, Robert Burgin and I arrived at the SHA headquarters in Cambridge for what we thought was to be a routine meeting with Keith Pearson and Neil McKay. At this meeting they told us that they were suspending their support for our scheme, as they had received information from Gareth that they had devised a plan which would incorporate Papworth into Cambridge University Hospitals and be significantly cheaper than our separate build. Our protestations that our scheme had an impeccable audit trail, and had recently passed a very tough Treasury-sponsored independent review, fell on deaf ears.

I was furious that Papworth had been treated so discourteously but, realising that the SHA would not budge, decided that my colleagues and I needed to meet with Gareth as a matter of urgency. As if this wasn't bad enough, Neil McKay also said that he wanted another independent assessment of our clinical activity projections. This was only four months after they had received his SHA's approval, following the previous independent assessment undertaken 12 months earlier.

Back in my office I sent Gareth Goodier a brief email insisting that I be afforded the courtesy of being briefed on this CUH generated Plan B, and the details underpinning it. Gareth despatched Stephen Graves, his director of corporate development, to come and brief us two days later.

I had first met Stephen Graves 14 years earlier, and he was probably the best informed CUH manager on our project. At the meeting, at which I was joined by Ken Brewer and David Stone, our recently appointed medical director, Stephen, explained that Cambridge University Hospitals had worked up some plans, in outline only, for the relocation of their accident and emergency department, ICU and a new children's hospital on land adjacent to their Rosie Maternity Hospital.

They had allocated a space for new Papworth, but it was some 7,000 square metres – or 20% smaller – than our plans, which had only just been reduced in order to pass the Treasury-sponsored Department of Health review. Stephen Graves acknowledged that their Plan B was at least two years behind our project, but they believed it would cost £30 million less than our greenfield option.

I was very sceptical that the commissioners would support a bid for a children's hospital, and the land they wanted was currently housing a mental health facility, operated by a neighbouring NHS trust, who had not been consulted. My 31 years of NHS experience told me that Plan B was unlikely to get off the ground and, if it did, it was at least four years, not two years, behind where our project was currently placed.

At the time I (wrongly) thought that this Plan B, promoted by CUH, may have arisen because of a sharp exchange of words between our two chairs at the stakeholder meeting held a few weeks earlier, on 16th July. During this meeting, Mary Archer had voiced her doubts about Papworth's ability to get ultimate approval for our greenfield option, and said she could not understand why we did not prepare a joint proposal with CUH. Robert Burgin rebuffed her claims with vigour, and so another meeting, where our two chairmen went head-to-head, came to an abrupt end. Also at the meeting was Chris Banks, the recently appointed CEO of the local primary care trust, formerly CEO of Peterborough Hospital, where he had steered their PFI project through to 'Financial Close'. After the meeting, Chris told me he was disappointed at the tone of the discussions, and naturally he would have given that feedback to Neil McKay at the SHA.

I met with Gareth Goodier early the following week, and his version of events was that he was asked by Bill Moyes, the executive chairman of Monitor, and Neil McKay to 'factor in' space for Papworth into the plans Gareth had mentioned to both of them, i.e. for a children's hospital, and accident and emergency department, etc. Apparently, both Bill Moyes and Neil McKay had interpreted the wording of the Department of Health approval letter sent to me in June as only lukewarm support, hence justifying their actions to ask Gareth to look at a Plan B.

Gareth also reiterated his request that I transfer the heart attack service to CUH, even though it had only been up and running at Papworth for a few months. Given that CUH were already short of space, and their finances were in bad shape, I took his comments to be aspirational, as there were no detailed plans in place. Knowing the 'Addenbrooke's culture' as I did, over the previous 19 years new ideas took a lot longer to introduce than at Papworth, partly due to size and partly due to the 'if it wasn't invented here, then we don't want it' syndrome. I said that we should ask our two medical directors to work up a plan, knowing that this would have more chance of success, and knew that they would remain faithful to the recently updated clinical vision document, which CUH clinicians had helped to write and signed up to.

The next day, 1st August, my chairman and I had a pre-arranged meeting with Bill Moyes and his senior colleagues at Monitor. Bill got straight to the point, saying that Gareth Goodier had told him that Addenbrooke's had a Plan B for Papworth which was £30 million cheaper than our greenfield option, and which he had briefed Neil McKay on. Bill Moyes then handed us copies of two letters he had sent to Gareth Goodier and Neil McKay – the first letter, he said, effectively telling Gareth to "put up or shut up."

It read:

"Dear Gareth,

I am writing to you following your comments to me as to the potential for Addenbrooke's to provide or host some or all of the services which are proposed to be provided in the future by Papworth, following the development of its PFI funded hospital.

As you are aware, Monitor's role is to consider the affordability of any proposed PFI scheme, taking account of activity level assumptions as confirmed by the SHA and relevant PCTs, and other matters which may impact on financial risk. Clearly, given the proximity of Addenbrooke's to the proposed site and your comments on services, it is relevant in considering these proposals to understand potential competition, and to the extent there are resultant concerns as to the affordability and risk of the scheme, any alternative options which should be considered by Papworth's board.

We are due to consider Papworth's PFI-funded proposals over the next few weeks. To the extent you have considered and prepared more detailed plans and scenarios for the alternative provision of these services, it would be timely to share these at the earliest opportunity with the SHA, who we understand to be considering its longer term commissioning models, and with Monitor.

William Moyes
Chairman."

Bill Moyes' letter to Neil McKay proved that the latter had raised doubts about our scheme two weeks before the stakeholder meeting of 16th July. The letter read as follows:

"Dear Neil,

I refer to your letter dated 2 July and our subsequent conversation on 10 July. You have expressed concerns that the proposals made by Papworth as to its PFI-funded scheme may not deliver the best outcome for services and could be more expensive than alternatives. We understand that Addenbrooke's have indicated that they may be in a position to provide the services from existing or lower cost facilities than those envisaged under the PFI scheme. I have written separately to Addenbrooke's to request them to provide more details as to their proposals.

We expect Papworth to be in a position to provide us with their detailed PFI models for our review over the next few weeks. We will perform this review in accordance with the advice (Roles and responsibilities in the approval of NHS foundation trust PFI schemes) which was published on 15 June 2007 jointly by the Department of Health and Monitor. To the extent our review indicates that the proposal may introduce an unacceptable level of risk, we are likely to press Papworth to think again about the scheme. We understand that Papworth aim to submit their Outline Business Case to the Department of Health (to consider the possible issue of a deed of safeguard by HM Treasury) during November.

If our review demonstrates an unacceptable level of financial risk, it is very unlikely that a deed of safeguard will be issued by HMT. But, it is not Monitor's role to consider it unacceptable or otherwise for Papworth to continue to be separate from a major secondary/tertiary care centre. For so long as Papworth complies with its Authorisation now and in the future, it will remain for its board to decide whether it continues to operate as an independent entity or whether the interests of its patients would be best served by a change in its status.

I think we are agreed that the SHA's role with regard to the proposed PFI is to consider and confirm forecast activity levels. My understanding is that the position of the SHA was set out in the letter dated 5 April 2007 from your director of commissioning, which states that not only does the SHA support the planning assumption in Papworth's proposals in terms of activity and finance, but also, more generally, the PFI scheme and its contribution to the delivery of the wider strategic aims of the local health community. This is not a position which I have gleaned from our conversations to date. I should be grateful to understand whether the SHA's views as to commissioning intentions and future purchasing models has changed since the date of that letter. If this is the case, it would be very helpful to understand your latest thinking before we conclude our review of Papworth's proposal. It may be, of course, that the SHA will not reach a final view until Sir Ara Darzi's work has been completed and considered.

If you wish to discuss any of the above, I should be happy to do so.

William Moyes
Chairman."

Bill Moyes was characteristically blunt with us, telling us that he had fought hard to maintain the freedoms of foundation trusts, and he expected us to push back hard at the SHA if they overstepped the mark regarding our proposed PFI scheme.

All well and good, I thought, but our new hospital was too important a project to see it fall because of a spat over foundation trust freedoms, which, as with the first wave of NHS trusts in the early 1990s, had seen most of their 'freedoms' watered down within a couple of years after having been granted.

The Papworth issue was an early event of the turf war between Monitor and the East of England SHA, which was to escalate over the coming months.

Meanwhile, our project director Ken Brewer and I worked closely with colleagues at Cambridge to examine the assumptions underpinning their Plan B, and hence the costs of that option. I was determined to ensure that we moved from the current 'apples and pears' comparison, to 'an apples and apples' one. At times like this I despaired for the future of the NHS finances, when outline assumptions such as those contained in the Cambridge University Hospital's proposal were given as much credibility as our scheme, which had an impeccable audit trail going back years.

In parallel with the assessment of capital costs, work was also underway on rechecking Papworth's patient activity projections. An excellent piece of work was carried out by Stephen Green, a senior member of National Director for Heart Disease Dr Roger Boyle's team. The outcome of their work was to endorse Papworth's projections, based on the very large population growth predicted for the east of England.

In November 2007, Papworth once again found itself in the headlines for the wrong reasons. A few days after the Maidstone and Tunbridge Wells Hospital MRSA issue broke, where several patient deaths were attributed to poor NHS care, our medical director, David Stone, received a call from Chief Medical Officer, Professor Sir Liam Donaldson. He asked us to 'pause' our lung transplant programme, as our recently submitted data to the Department of Health had flagged up a higher than predicted 30-day post-operative mortality rate, with seven deaths following the 21 most recent operations.

A couple of days later the media descended on us in force, scenting another NHS scandal. I gave several interviews to national TV, press, and the *Today* programme on Radio Four. I felt it only right that I should lead from the front, and take any flak that was hurled in our direction.

During this pause in our lung transplant programme I attended the annual CEO conference in London. As he arrived to give the keynote address, David Nicholson, now CEO of the NHS, made a beeline for me and asked if there was anything he should know about our situation.

He was clearly under intense pressure because of the Maidstone and Tunbridge Wells problem. I told him that I genuinely believed that our problem was largely down to complex medical complications in a low-volume, high-risk area of surgery, but did not want to convey an air of complacency.

Back at Papworth, the Healthcare Commission were able to conclude their investigation within two weeks, due in no small part to the excellent data kept by the transplant directorate (a hallmark of this service, stemming from the need to prove its effectiveness when it was first set up by Terence English back in the 1970s), and the excellent leadership of the current transplant director, Steven Tsui.

The Healthcare Commission's report complimented Papworth on the actions we had taken leading up to the 'pause', and made several recommendations which we fully accepted. The lung transplant service resumed immediately, and over the coming years achieved some of the best results of any centre in the world.

With this episode concluded, I was able to give my full attention to getting our OBC out of the doldrums. Following further detailed discussions with Cambridge University Hospitals, David Stone, Ken Brewer and myself were invited to attend their board meeting in early December. Following an analysis of the assumptions underpinning Plan B, it was agreed to send a statement to the SHA and Monitor. This statement was to inform them that there was no difference in capital cost between the two options, i.e. Papworth's greenfield and CUH's Plan B. This confirmation was reaffirmed in a letter to me from Mary Archer and Stephen Graves (deputising for Gareth Goodier who was in Australia on leave).

I heard nothing from the SHA, and ruefully concluded that the events of the past five months, and the delay it had caused, were an inevitable result of the several changes in their leadership, with the consequential loss of organisational memory.

CHAPTER SEVENTEEN

2008-10

Decision-makers' Dither

The year 2008 started with Monitor commencing their Affordability Review of our scheme. The results of this were conveyed to us in a four-page letter in mid-April. As accounting officer, Monitor placed the responsibility on me to advise the board as to whether the risks involved in proceeding to the next stage had been sufficiently taken into account.

I had little fear of complying with this requirement, as our three chairmen had been scrupulous in making sure we had an excellent audit trail on this complex, controversial subject. At our April board meeting we unanimously agreed to proceed and advertise the scheme in the *OJEU*. I wrote to Bill Moyes at Monitor to inform him, and his reply of 27th May was typically robust, stressing the need for us to pass the 'downside scenario' test, and then signing off by reminding me in no uncertain terms that it was down to me to tell Neil

McKay at the SHA not to overstep the mark in their role in this project.

The final paragraph of Bill Moyes' letter read as follows:

> *"We also expressed our disappointment and concern as to the current level of involvement of the SHA in the scheme. We would strongly encourage the trust to ensure that each party fulfils only the roles set out in guidance issued on 15 June 2007, 'Roles and Responsibilities in the Approval of NHS Foundation Trust PFI Schemes'. A failure to do this risks confusion and ultimately may put the trust's board in an untenable position."*

Away from the high stakes politics of NHS management, it was nice to host a visit from Chief Medical Officer, Professor Sir Liam Donaldson, who was kind enough to pay us a visit and thank our transplant team, in particular, for their superb handling of the events seven months earlier. Following his visit he wrote:

> *"Dear Stephen,*
>
> *Thank you for hosting my recent visit to Papworth Hospital. I was deeply impressed with the work and the achievements of you and your team over many years.*

> *Please convey my thanks to those who gave their time to meet with me yesterday. Their willingness to deal with the difficult challenges they recently faced sensibly and calmly, to help ensure the best possible outcomes for patients, was admirable."*

The SHA finally gave our OBC their official endorsement, and the remainder of 2008 was taken up with the lengthy and bureaucratic process of advertising in the *OJEU*. To complete this, however, we needed Department of Health approval and, once again, our requests for sign off were greeted with a deafening silence. This time it was down to the escalating financial problems caused by the Peterborough Hospital PFI scheme and severe financial problems at Hinchingbrooke Hospital.

Neil McKay told me that David Nicholson, CEO of the NHS, was very worried that Cambridgeshire and Peterborough was a financial 'basket case', and until matters improved they could not be seen to approve another PFI scheme in this county. Despite arguing that only 17% of Papworth's income came from Cambridgeshire, we were clearly in the wrong place at the wrong time.

Months went by with no progress, but then in June 2009, on a glorious, sunny evening at the top of the BT Tower in London at an event organised by the NHS Confederation, I ambushed Andy Burnham, the recently appointed secretary of state for health.

After he had finished his official duties, there was the usual melee of people queuing up to speak to him before he made his exit. I managed to get my slot, and after introducing myself, he replied, "Have you heard of a pop group called Half Man Half Biscuit?" I replied that I had, as I was a regular listener of the John Peel radio programme. He told me they had recorded a song about Papworth Hospital, as the father of one of the band members had undergone a heart transplant there. I asked him if he was able to allow our PFI scheme to proceed to the next stage, given the extensive due diligence it had already undergone. In reply, he said to "drop him a line and he would look into it".

Despite the positive tone of our conversation, nothing transpired, and 2009 gave way to 2010, with a General Election only months away. The number of PFI schemes being approved slowed to a trickle but, just as in 2004, we hoped for a pre-election largesse, with our scheme getting the green light.

In January 2010, the Regius Professor of Physic, Patrick Sissons and I wrote to Andy Burnham outlining the huge potential of the Cambridge Biomedical Campus, and the important role that a relocated Papworth Hospital could play. We wrote:

> *"During these past five years developments in Cambridge have enabled collaboration between the University, the NHS and the life sciences and bio-tech industries, which help the UK to*

remain internationally competitive in these sectors [...] Over £200 million of public money has been invested in improving the transport infrastructure, and several thousand new homes are to be built in the area over the next decade. The move of Papworth Hospital is therefore part of a very important capital investment and job creation programme for the Cambridge sub-region and the country."

We did not get a reply.

In February, however, I received a reply to an earlier letter of mine, from Sir David Nicholson. He said that progress was in the hands of the Treasury, but that he would let me know if matters progressed.

Later that month Vice Chancellor of the University of Cambridge, Professor Alison Richards, also wrote to Andy Burnham, reinforcing the research benefits that a Papworth move to the Cambridge Biomedical Campus would bring.

Again, a deafening silence.

In March 2010, the King's Fund, the independent health charity and think tank ran a series of events at which the health leaders of the three main political parties would outline their manifestos for the coming General Election and then take questions from the floor. Normally, it is the best course of action to keep a low profile during election periods, given the intense scrutiny the NHS finds itself under, but as the stakes were so high,

I decided to attend the Andy Burnham session and see if I could grab a word with him.

It was Wednesday 31st March, and once again I managed to manoeuvre my way to the front of the queue to question the health secretary. This time I greeted him with the words, "Hello, it is Half Man Half Biscuit from Papworth Hospital here." Although he was momentarily nonplussed, he quickly recovered and told me that he had signed our scheme off that very day.

Back in the office the next morning, Thursday 1st April, I took a call from Neil McKay, congratulating me on getting to go-ahead – he having been informed by the Department of Health. As the next day was Good Friday, I went home that evening feeling that our hard work and perseverance was, at long last, paying off.

On the next working day following Easter, Tuesday 6th April, Prime Minister Gordon Brown called the date for the General Election. At first I did not think this would affect our PFI scheme, as approval to advertise in the *Official Journal of the European Union* had, in other projects, not been considered a significant act, and hence permissible in the period of 'purdah'. Later that morning, however, I received a call from the PFI unit at the Department of Health telling me that our project had been 'caught up' in the Easter break, and had not been signed off by Treasury before the election was called. Therefore, we could not proceed, and would have to await the outcome of the General Election.

To put it mildly, I was devastated, as another lengthy delay seemed inevitable, with possible terminal consequences for the scheme.

All of our efforts seemed wasted. Over the previous few weeks I had received several phone calls from Andrew Lansley, promising to press Andy Burnham into signing off the scheme. Ironically, given what was to transpire two months later, he only got around to writing to Mr Burnham on 6th April, the day the election was called.

Sadly, this was a case of too little too late.

In the run up to the election, Andrew Lansley publicly stated on several occasions that getting the move of Papworth Hospital to the Cambridge Biomedical Campus was one of his top five priorities, should he become secretary of state for health.

Two weeks after the election, with Andrew now in place as secretary of state for health, I received phone calls from two local Conservative councillors who thought I should know that, at a recent private meeting, Andrew Lansley had gone noticeably quiet when they asked him about the Papworth move.

I was grateful for their courtesies, but thought nothing of this at the time.

On Thursday 19th June, after I had finished my meeting with Gareth Goodier, I bumped into Mary Archer in the main corridor at Addenbrooke's. She enquired as to the progress of our scheme, and then went on to say something which I took to be small talk, but which took on a whole different meaning 36 hours later.

Mary said that she understood that Simon Burns, the MP for Chelmsford and number two to Lansley at the Department of Health, was in charge of the PFI projects, and that if we had any further problems to let her know, as her husband Jeffrey frequently lunched with Simon Burns. I thought it a slightly odd statement, and thanked Mary. Perhaps this was the way to get things done, but I was confident that our scheme would be allowed to proceed, as Andrew Lansley now had his dream job as secretary of state for health, and could ensure that no further unnecessary obstacles were placed in our way.

The next evening, Friday 20th June, there was a dinner at a Cambridge college for local NHS chairs, CEOs and medical directors, celebrating the end of a successful series of lectures and seminars, organised by the Cambridgeshire and Peterborough NHS foundation trust. The guest of honour was Andrew Lansley, who, after a brief speech, left the top table and came and sat down next to me at one of the other tables. I introduced him to several colleagues, but could tell he wanted a private word with me, so we shuffled along to the end of the long bench table.

Over the next five minutes he told me that he could not help with progressing our scheme, saying that Cabinet protocol prevented this and that I should deal with his deputy, Simon Burns. He then said that if I had any difficulty in accessing Mr Burns that I should contact Jeffrey Archer, via Mary Archer, who would act as an intermediary.

I could not believe what I was hearing. I had known Andrew for 14 years, and believed that he was sincere when he said that he would do all that he could to help Papworth get the new hospital we desperately needed. To suggest that I use Lord Archer as an intermediary, somebody I had never met, and was clearly part of a previous generation of Conservative politicians, seemed weird, and slightly furtive.

I did not know whether to laugh or cry.

I suggested to Andrew that he should have a word with Robert Burgin, our chairman, who was looking on with great curiosity from the top table.

I took my leave from an otherwise enjoyable evening at Corpus Christi College. Whilst driving home, all I could think of was why Andrew, an experienced politician, had not known of this problem before making promises over several years to "sort the Papworth issue".

The next afternoon Robert Burgin rang me and asked if I, too, had had a strange conversation with Andrew Lansley. We compared notes, and concluded that we had both received the polite brush off.

After several more weeks haggling with the Department of Health's PFI, we were informed that our scheme could proceed, and advertise for companies to build the proposed new hospital in the *Official Journal of the European Union*, which we did in August 2010.

At the closing date of 31st October, we had received six firm expressions of interest. This list was then whittled down to three major construction firms: Bouygues, John Laing and Skanska.

The next six months involved a lot of detailed activity between the three bidders and Papworth's clinical design teams. Dozens of meetings were held to ensure that these three companies had enough information so as to come up with their best designs.

CHAPTER EIGHTEEN

2011

"Stop The Project; Merge With Your London Counterpart"

In June 2011, after very detailed consideration, and working closely with our professional advisers, our board decided to select Bouygues and Skanska to go forward into the 'Competitive Dialogue' stage, aka appointment business case (ABC) stage of the complex PFI procurement process.

Then, in the following month, July 2011, yet another major threat to our scheme arose. This time, the CEO of Cambridge University Hospitals, Gareth Goodier, informed me of another of his 'great ideas'. He proposed that Papworth, CUH and the Royal Brompton and Harefield hospitals should combine our respective transplant services and build a Transplant Institute on the Cambridge Biomedical Campus. This idea might have appeared attractive in normal circumstances, but under the rules of PFI, it constituted a significant alteration to the brief given to our two bidders, and could give the Department of Health reason to halt our whole project.

I assumed that Gareth had been approached by Bob Bell, the Canadian CEO at the Royal Brompton and Harefield NHS trust. In my meetings with Bob, he had suggested that his trust was thinking of capitalising on the huge value of their Brompton site in Chelsea, southwest London, and build a new hospital elsewhere. I had never envisaged that Cambridge was on their list of possible sites, whether that be for the whole of their trust, or just the transplant service.

Only recently I had given my full support to Gareth's idea of building a private hospital, and also to Mary Archer's request that Papworth participate in a reactivated project to build an education centre, both of which were to be on the Cambridge Biomedical Campus. I felt that these proposals should be worked up fully before we set off on any more initiatives.

With regard to the proposed private hospital, Gareth told me that he was in advanced discussions with a Japanese company. The problem was that their only hospital in Europe was in Sofia, Bulgaria. He asked me if I would ask some of my doctors to go there and assess the quality of their hospital. I persuaded two of our cardiologists, Len Shapiro and Simon Fynn, and our cardiac surgeon, David Jenkins, to undertake this task, and to report back with their findings.

My three colleagues agreed to spend a few days in Bulgaria, and reported back to me, giving a balanced view of a good standard of clinical care, but admitted to being slightly alarmed at the notice inside the hospital entrance asking people to 'leave their firearms at the reception desk'!

Gareth pushed ahead with his idea, which soon expanded to include a hotel and, along with the education centre, became known as the Forum Project. Seven years later, the Forum Project had not progressed, and was finally killed off by the Board of Cambridge University Hospitals in 2018.

Although I did not think that the 'three trust Transplant Institute' idea would fly, I was concerned lest the SHA and Monitor behave as they had done in 2007(when CUH proposed their Plan B option), and place our project on hold until the viability of this new idea was checked. To avoid this happening, I decided to go and see the CEO of the only other hospital contemplating a similar idea.

Therefore, I visited Newcastle Hospital, and asked Sir Len Fenwick, their veteran CEO, what their Transplant Institute would comprise. The visit to Newcastle confirmed my previously held views that the actual content of any such building should allow usage by other related clinical specialties, given the irregular nature of transplant activity. The clinical model introduced by Terence English at Papworth in 1979 was still valid 31 years later: a dedicated unit for transplantation would not be cost effective; the best model was to use existing facilities, such as operating theatres and intensive care beds, so as to maximise the utilisation of these high-cost facilities.

I reported my findings from Newcastle to Gareth, but he was not to be deterred.

Things went quiet for a few weeks, and then Bob Bell rang me to tell me that he and his chairman, Sir Robert Finch, were keen to add Cambridge onto their list of options for the new location for the whole of Royal Brompton Hospital, and not just a Transplant Institute.

Not for the first time in my career, I was told I needed to 'see the big picture'. My feet were firmly on the ground, and I was determined not to let this crazy option - in effect, a stalking horse option of moving to Cambridge - unravel the stakeholder support for our move to the Cambridge Biomedical Campus, that we had carefully built and maintained over the previous decade.

It felt like we were playing a game of Snakes and Ladders, my estimate being that we were currently 70% there, but one false move would see us tumbling down a snake, back to the low 30s or, worse still, out of the game altogether, given the parlous financial state of the NHS in eastern England.

Yet again our project was facing a situation of 'not letting the facts get in the way of a good story', so I decided that Papworth should embark upon a multi-pronged rebuttal of this latest in a long line of threats to derail our move to Cambridge.

I felt that I could cut through the spin and prove that the Royal Brompton, like Papworth, received a comparatively small amount of its income from its highly specialised services. I would pose the question: Why would patients want to make a 100-mile roundtrip to Cambridge, when there are six other excellent cardiothoracic centres in London?

My other line of rebuttal was to ask Regius Professor of Physic, Patrick Sissons, who was also quasi CEO of our Academic Health Science Centre, known as Cambridge University Health Partners, to look into the research and educational benefits this 'big idea' would generate.

Patrick briefed newly installed Vice Chancellor, Professor Sir Leszek Borysiewicz, a qualified doctor who had previously worked in Cambridge, including participation in the transplant services at CUH and Papworth. Who better then to assess the merits, or otherwise, of the ideas emerging from the Royal Brompton Hospital, and enthusiastically supported by their 'ambassador', i.e. former CEO Gareth Goodier?

I delivered the results of my patient flow analysis for the Royal Brompton Hospital to Gareth in a letter on 9th September and sent a more detailed analysis to Bob Bell on 19th September. As I expected, they both rejected my conclusions, which were as follows:

- 88% of patients lived within a 25-mile radius of the Royal Brompton Hospital, and so the overwhelming majority would choose to be treated at the other major cardiothoracic centres in London, rather than incur the inconvenience and cost of a 100-mile roundtrip to Cambridge;

- However, assuming that 20% of patients would be happy to transfer their treatment to a new hospital in Cambridge, particularly those patients with rare, highly specialised needs, then this would only need 60 beds, to meet this demand;
- And of the 20% of patients who might make the trip to Cambridge, 71% of them were in the specialty of respiratory medicine, with only 6% in cardiac surgery.

Bob Bell responded, setting out the Royal Brompton's position in a joint letter to Gareth and myself on 22nd September. He set the scene as follows:

> *"For the last eight months our board and senior executive team have been involved in a process that, with the help of external advice, has been developing and then evaluating a set of strategic options for the trust, one of which has been this proposition. The expenditure of time and effort in this process has been significant – you will have seen evidence of this not merely in the minutes of our debates on this topic during our board meetings but also in terms of the visit by several of our non-executives to the Addenbrooke's campus. Indeed, my chairman has already*

> *mentioned in an email to Dr Archer and in a conversation with Mr Robert Burgin that moving RBH to Cambridge is a preferred option of some of our board members [...] at this stage, we are not prepared to speculate on activity levels.*
>
> *We are not timewasters, nor do we expect you to be.*
>
> *Equally, we would not pretend that relocation to Cambridge is our only option. Indeed, we continue to explore how we could rebuild our RBH campus on another site sympathetic to our many confluent interests with Imperial College."*

The due diligence undertaken by the University of Cambridge also led them to conclude that the risks that this plan posed for the relocation of Papworth Hospital outweighed the stated advantages. A letter from the vice chancellor to the chairman of the Royal Brompton, Sir Robert Finch, confirming this view was sent in November 2011.

Eight years later, the Royal Brompton Hospital has still not made a final decision as to where they plan to relocate to.

Back in the real world, 2011 ended with Papworth once again in the headlines, not just in the UK but internationally. The reason for this was the emergency admission of His Royal Highness Prince Phillip, on 23rd December. He underwent primary angioplasty and was successfully discharged a couple of days after Boxing Day.

This hectic period began for me at 6.30pm on Friday 23rd December. I was getting ready to go home when I took a call from Consultant Cardiologist Dr Sarah Clarke, who told me that Prince Phillip was en route to Papworth in a RAF helicopter. I realised that the media and the police would descend on the place in large numbers, so I contacted my executive colleagues and we soon activated our plans for such an event. I was surprised that Buckingham Palace had released a press statement whilst Prince Phillip was still in the air, giving us little time to get the non-clinical arrangements in place.

My achievement was to persuade our six catering staff not to close at 7pm, even though two of them told me it would mean them having to forego their Friday night bingo session. I asked Sean, our head cook, what food he could rustle up, and one hour later the delicious smell of curry was wafting out of the canteen, and gratefully received by the media and police, who knew they were going to be in for a long night.

A couple of weeks later, Sir Neil McKay told me that he was in a pub with Sir David Nicholson when they saw the Sky News story breaking, and he rang my office to wish me good luck. I missed the call – no doubt I was checking on the progress of the curry!

CHAPTER NINETEEN

2012-13

Stop the Project; Move to Peterborough

The year 2012 was characterised by extreme nervousness at the SHA and the Department of Health over the escalating deficit at Peterborough Hospital. In this climate they would not be approving any more PFI schemes in Cambridgeshire for the foreseeable future. Behind the scenes, however, the picture for us was not so bleak, as discussions with DH officials resulted in their agreement to provide us with loans at very low rates of interest. They also promised a 'bullet payment', or grant, for the cost of purchasing the eight acres of land on the Cambridge Biomedical Campus.

This would mean that the PFI deal we were seeking would only amount to circa 56% of the total capital cost, and due to the advantageous financial climate prevailing at that time, and the recent improvements made to PFI by Treasury, it was shaping up to be one of the best PFI deals ever struck in the NHS. I took every opportunity

I could to convey my views to DH officials that this was a very safe scheme as if, in the unlikely scenario Papworth ran out of work, the facilities would be used by Cambridge University Hospitals whose estate needed major investment.

As 2012 ticked by we came to realise that the other side of the coin of the recent Treasury review of PFI was the introduction of more stages for regulatory approval. We were stuck in the newly termed 'appointment business case' stage, and needed to close what was now called 'Competitive Dialogue', and select one of the two companies still in the frame and enter the 'preferred bidder' stage. Theoretically, we could trigger this without ministerial approval, but that would put into jeopardy the attractive financial package we had negotiated with the Department of Health.

In June, in response to a letter from our chairman, Robert Burgin, urging the DH to allow our scheme to progress, Una O'Brien, the permanent secretary, in her response wrote:

> *"My understanding is that the SHA's sign off of the trust's business case has been delayed because of a new strategic review needed as a consequence of the problems at Peterborough, and their decision whether to sign off (a necessary step prior to any approval by the Department) is unlikely to come until July. However I can assure you that once the SHA have released the business case, officials*

here will work with you to progress your project through to completion."

Despite their previous hostility towards each other, Monitor and our SHA seemed to have 'buried the hatchet'. They sent me a letter to inform me that they had recently met and agreed that a further review of our patient activity projections was necessary. They agreed that Deloitte should carry out this work, the third such independent review in four years.

Once again, our patient activity projections were endorsed, and in some areas considered to be too conservative. Monitor then passed the ball to the SHA, stating they would only carry out their latest Affordability Review after the SHA had signed these off, including the financial implications for every commissioner, i.e. primary care trust, under their jurisdiction. The problem was that the SHA was under strict instructions from Sir David Nicholson to do no such thing, at least not until the Parliamentary Public Accounts Committee hearing into the Peterborough PFI scheme, and the Hinchingbrooke Hospital/Circle franchise deal had taken place. Unfortunately, this PAC hearing was not scheduled to take place until the autumn.

This constant delay made both of our bidders very anxious, and there was no certainty that their bosses in France and Sweden might not decide to cut their losses and walk away from our scheme.

At our September 2012 board meeting we had a long and detailed discussion as to the risks we faced. On the one hand, we could placate the bidders and put one of them out of their misery by moving to preferred bidder stage. On the other hand, what retaliatory action would we face from the Department of Health and Monitor if we took such action? We felt that we were 'damned if we do, damned if we don't'.

Immediately after this board meeting, Robert Burgin wrote again to the DH, but this time to the minister responsible for PFI schemes, Earl Howe. His reply, received one month later, said:

> *"There is a risk in the trust closing its Competitive Dialogue and seeking final bids. Were the (Monitor/SHA) review to indicate a need for significant changes to the scheme's specifications, it would be difficult and expensive to alter the procurement to respond to these. Therefore, while I understand your and the trust's frustration, I would not be in favour of closure of Competitive Dialogue at this point.*
>
> *I know you will find this reply disappointing, but the best course of action would be for you to keep in dialogue with the SHA. Until they have completed their review, I am afraid that the Department cannot agree to you closing the dialogue."*

In December 2012, Neil McKay told me that the SHA intended to give us their support as soon as the heat had died down from the recent Public Accounts Committee hearing. Despite feeling let down by Neil over his actions in 2007, when he supported the Cambridge University Hospitals Plan B fiasco, I believed I could trust him and his colleagues to do the right thing as one of their final acts before they were abolished as part of the Lansley reforms of the NHS, coming into force on 1st April 2013.

So, at their board meeting in January 2013, the SHA took their last big decision and approved (on behalf of the commissioning authorities, i.e. the primary care trusts, the patient activity projections and their financial consequences) of the move of Papworth Hospital to the Cambridge Biomedical Campus.

Neil rang to tell me of their decision, but the pleasure of hearing that news was overshadowed by an email I received two hours later from the Department of Health. This was a pre-emptive strike on their part, warning me not to advise my board to close the Competitive Dialogue stage.

Monitor contacted me a couple of weeks later, setting out the details of their latest Affordability Review. They said that although the SHA decision was important, upon reflection they had decided that I now needed to get updated confirmation from the new commissioning authorities, called Clinical Commissioning Groups (CCG).

I set about making contact with the plethora of new NHS organisations taking the stage from 1st April 2013. This latest NHS reorganisation, the ninth in my 37-year career, was, in the words of Sir David Nicholson, "so big that you can see it from Mars."

Understandably, the new CCGs did not have the move of Papworth to the Cambridge Biomedical Campus as the number one item on their agendas, but over the next three months I managed to secure the support of our main commissioners to sign up to the financial implications that their predecessor, primary care trusts, had previously agreed.

Once this task had been achieved, we felt that as long as we passed Monitor's latest Affordability Review that the Department of Health, and ultimately, Treasury, would do the decent thing and let our scheme proceed to the preferred bidder stage, which in normal circumstances would have happened 12 months earlier.

Clearly, I was too naive.

Just when we thought we had weathered all of the storms, there emerged yet another major threat to our scheme.

The review of the Peterborough Hospital PFI scheme, ordered by the Department of Health in the wake of the highly critical Public Accounts Committee report, was to be much wider than we had at first envisaged. In an effort to restore some credibility, it soon became obvious that the Department of Health had instructed one of the Big Four consultancy firms, PwC, to come up with some radical ideas to solve the financial crisis at Peterborough.

'Find a solution . . . any solution' should have been the title of the Peterborough assignment!

What started out with a low-key conversation with the PwC partner leading this review, rapidly turned into possibly the biggest threat our project had faced in its nine-year struggle.

Initially, some of my colleagues at Papworth thought that I was exaggerating the threat that the Peterborough rescue project posed to us, but they soon accepted that my instincts were correct. In my book, thinking radically is fine, so long as there is some foundation of logic. That was not the way that this team from PwC appeared to want to run this project.

At my first attendance of the Operations and Finance Group held at Peterborough Hospital, there was a surreal atmosphere. Several young, earnest and no doubt very bright analysts were sitting away from the main table, typing into their laptops and asking questions which would not have been necessary had they done their homework and read the numerous papers that were in the public domain about the Cambridgeshire and Peterborough health economy.

The task for the representatives from local hospitals and commissioners was to discuss the merits of the long list of options, which were tabled. One option was to transfer part of Papworth's services to the fourth floor of Peterborough Hospital, currently being used as offices for administrative staff. Most of those present appeared to support my views on why that was clinically and financially a non-starter; but the meeting finished with the partner from PwC saying that the same list of options would be discussed at the forthcoming Clinical Advisory Group (CAG) meeting.

At the first CAG meeting, Papworth's clinical representative, Sarah Clarke, one of our senior consultant cardiologists, was astonished when the paper tabled had significantly altered the Papworth option so that it now proposed to move ALL of Papworth Hospital to Peterborough, and abandon the move to Cambridge.

Sarah reported back to me that this option had no support whatsoever from her fellow clinicians present at the meeting; but PwC appeared immune to the incredulous and negative reaction this option generated from all and sundry.

I could not believe the rank amateurism we were experiencing. The fourth floor of Peterborough Hospital was around 5,000 square metres, whilst the size of Papworth Hospital was 33,000 square metres. *Call me old-fashioned*, I thought, *but how did this option, on mathematical grounds alone, pass the in-house assurance test that these multi-million-pound-assignments were supposed to have built in*?

The second meeting of the Operations and Finance Group was held on 17th May 2013, this time chaired by the former finance director of the Northern Strategic Health Authority, Jane Tomkinson. She soon grasped how incensed I was at the inclusion of the Papworth option, and saved me the job of asking how the capital cost of £20 million had been arrived at for this option. The failure of the PwC team to give a satisfactory answer, I felt, left her feeling very unhappy at this option remaining on the table, but it would not have been appropriate for her to pursue her doubts in this forum.

As well as keeping my Papworth colleagues up to speed with this alarming development, I also briefed the Regius Professor of Physic, and the vice chancellor of the University of Cambridge. We wasted little time in writing to Jeremy Hunt, who had replaced Andrew Lansley as secretary of state for health. Our letter pointed out the importance of the Cambridge Biomedical Campus to UK health science and research, noting that Astra Zeneca had recently decided to move their global headquarters and major research hub to the Campus.

Mr Hunt's reply of 25th July stuck to the previous party line. He wrote:

> *"While I appreciate your concerns about the delay in approving the redevelopment of Papworth Hospital, you will be aware that some trusts which have undertaken major PFI projects in the past have subsequently run into financial problems, and it is important to avoid similar problems arising with new schemes."*

Such was the political pressure to find a solution to the Peterborough problem that months ticked by, with the Department of Health refusing to say if, or when, they would make a decision about our proposed PFI scheme.

Then, in late October, we heard that ministers had approved, 'in principle', our appointment business case, but they stressed that it was the Treasury who would decide if we could move into the confirmatory business case (CBC) stage, i.e. the final stage before Financial Close, by appointing the preferred bidder.

In normal circumstances, this would have been excellent news, but in reality it was the Department of Health 'passing the buck', as all the information I was receiving from local sources said that Treasury were refusing to give up on the 'Papworth at Peterborough' option.

Meanwhile, Papworth's chairman for the past eight years, Robert Burgin, in a mutual agreement with our Council of Governors, said that he would not seek another term of office. Both parties agreed that Papworth now needed a chairman with extensive NHS connections if we were to break the deadlock we were in with our PFI scheme. Robert's background was in the water and housing sector, and although I had persuaded our lead governor to defer pushing this idea to completion 12 months previously, the last year had convinced me that perhaps a change of chair would help us launch a lobbying campaign targeting different individuals in government. Furthermore, Monitor had recently issued new rules for terms of office of chairs, recommending that two terms of three years should become the norm. Once this decision was made, Robert wanted to bow out by helping us 'up the ante', and 'nudge' the Department of Health into acknowledging that we were within our rights to appoint the preferred bidder.

Following a full and positive discussion at our November 2013 board meeting, we concluded that the risk of one or both of our bidders walking away in frustration was now much greater than the impact of sanctions on us from the Department of Health. We decided, therefore, to complete the final evaluation of the bids from Bouygues and Skanska, and proceed to 'Mind to Appoint', in the parlance of the very cumbersome procurement rules for PFI schemes.

I subsequently wrote to Director General of Finance at the Department of Health, Richard Douglas, to inform him that our board had decided upon this course of action.

I wrote:

> *"At its meeting on Thursday 28th November, the board of directors decided that it is presently minded to appoint Skanska as its preferred bidder. Both bidders have been advised of this decision and have also been advised that the decision should not be considered as an award of preferred bidder status, which will only be granted following Department of Health and Treasury approval.*
>
> *The board took the decision to progress the procurement to this limited extent given:*
>
> - *The fact that the draft Appointment Business Case had been cleared by Department of Health and forwarded to Treasury;*

- *The need for the project to keep pace with other important projects on the Cambridge Biomedical Campus, including the relocation of Astra Zeneca;*
- *The need to minimise the continuing waste of public (and private sector) money resulting from the procurement delay."*

The expression, 'dancing on a pinhead' seemed most appropriate to describe this most delicate phase of our project, and bring to an end over 60 years of uncertainty as to the future of Papworth Hospital.

As I expected, I received a curt reply, which came within 24 hours, about 30 days quicker than the Department's normal response time. It said:

> *"Officials at the Department of Health, who were working on the approval of the business case, were in discussion with Monitor and Addenbrooke's to provide some assurances requested by the Treasury, and I am therefore extremely disappointed at the trust's decision to take this step, and to do so without any consultation with Department of Health officials.*
>
> *I must remind you that the draft appointment of Preferred Bidder Business Case is a key approval stage in the clearance of PFI projects. It is a stage at which, amongst other important considerations, the scheme's affordability is confirmed, and it is a key stage in*

the government's decision on whether the scheme may benefit from support in the form of a Deed of Safeguard which, as you know, provides comfort that lenders consider essential. Approval of PFI business cases is a joint decision between the Department of Health and Treasury, and consideration of Papworth's is still ongoing.

With this in mind, you and others in the trust's board of directors will need to consider very carefully the appropriateness of instigating any further expenditure either in the trust's own books or those of any contractor ahead of approval of the draft approval of Preferred Bidder Business Case, given that there is no guarantee that the scheme and its current scope will be approved and therefore benefit from a Deed of Safeguard.

In addition to any other matters that may be raised in the course of the Department's and Treasury's further consideration of the scheme, it will now be necessary for officials to look into the exact arrangements leading to the trust's effective closure of the scheme, to establish what precautions have been taken to ensure that any specification or contractual changes that may become necessary can be applied without loss of value for money, given that the competition is now effectively closed.

I have copied this letter to Matthew Style, Head of Health Spending at the Treasury, and

David Bennett at Monitor, as they too will need to consider the implications of the trust's actions.

Yours sincerely,

Richard."

It was a tour de force of official approbation, befitting someone of Richard's pedigree, having worked at the Department of Health for many years.

A few weeks later, having had time to reflect on the measured approach taken by Papworth, I received a further letter from Richard Douglas, again comprehensive, but less strident in tone, setting out a way ahead.

The key sections were as follows:

"The extracts that you have provided from the letters to each bidder provide some reassurance on the issue of exposure to costs, though I would be grateful if you could forward the full texts to Ben M for consideration by the Department's Private Finance Unit.

I am aware of the frustrations that the trust has had over the past few years in seeking approvals for its scheme. However, I would like to focus on the steps we have agreed with the Treasury, that now need to be taken for the government to be able to reach a decision on the business case. I understand that Ben M called you on Friday 6th December to give you notice of the next steps, but I am writing now to explain formally what will be required.

First of all, a follow-up review from Monitor will be required – essentially to ensure that reasonable steps have been put in place to address the risks identified in the financial review that Monitor undertook earlier this year.

The precise coverage and detail of the review will be for Monitor to determine, but in essence, the review will look into the following areas [...]"

The letter then listed the nine areas, covering patient activity assumptions, robustness of our cost improvement programme, confirmation of the £55 million loans and grants we had provisionally agreed from the foundation trust financing facility, downside scenarios, and last, but not least, Succession Planning at the trust.

I got the message.

His letter continued, and got more interesting:

"I have arranged with Monitor through Sir Bruce Keogh, for a short independent clinical review to be conducted which will be focused on the arguments for and against your proposals to locate the facility as planned next to Addenbrooke's Hospital, as well as a clinical review of the feasibility of the utilisation of any excess capacity at Peterborough.

The clinical review will be carried out by a clinician from another region with no connection to Papworth who will report back to the Department and Monitor.

In the current climate a PFI scheme cannot be approved to proceed to selection of Preferred Bidder without these questions having been answered to a high degree of assurance.

I have copied this letter to Miranda Carter and Martin Smith (Monitor) who will ensure that these two additional pieces of review work are instigated when they see your response.

I understand that this additional analysis will not be welcomed, but I would be grateful if you could acknowledge this letter and make arrangements with the Monitor team for this work to be carried out."

As we expected, the steps included yet another Affordability Review by Monitor, and other requirements, presumably at the behest of Treasury. Noting that one of the conditions was 'succession planning at the trust', I assumed this was a gentle reminder to me that my style of management may be reaching its sell-by date, and a more subservient, or in 'Department speak', corporate style, would be appreciated by the centre.

Whatever these organisations thought of me, I was determined to see this important project through to its successful completion.

CHAPTER TWENTY

2014

It's Not What You Know, It's Who You Know

In January 2014, in one of his final duties as chairman, Robert Burgin and I met with Julian Huppert, the Liberal Democrat MP for Cambridge City constituency. We had heard that Julian was a friend of the special political adviser (SPAD), to Danny Alexander, the Liberal Democrat chief secretary to the Treasury, and number two to Chancellor of the Exchequer George Osborne.

Julian said he was happy to help. We replied by saying that we wanted to bypass the officials and get these two politicians to acknowledge the importance to the wider Cambridge scene, and help to get our move to Cambridge moving again.

One of Robert's last acts as chairman, in deciding to meet with Julian, turned out to be a masterstroke, as events over the next few months would prove.

Meanwhile, I had replied to Richard Douglas requesting a meeting so that he could meet our new chairman, taking over from Robert on 1st February – a certain John Wallwork.

John had retired from Papworth Hospital in 2011, but he continued to work for the hospital charity in a part-time capacity. He was charged with cultivating potential high-worth donors, especially those who might be interested in making significant financial contributions to our fundraising appeal to build the Heart and Lung Research Institute. Following Robert Burgin's decision to step down, John emerged as a serious contender to become our next chairman.

Richard Douglas agreed to my request for a meeting, and this was held at Richmond House on Friday 31st January 2014. Representing the Treasury was Matthew Style, deputy director of Public Services, and from Monitor, Martin Smith and Miranda Carter.

Matthew stressed that the large deficit at Peterborough Hospital was a major embarrassment for the government, and how important it was, therefore, that a solution to be found as a matter of urgency, even if that meant 'changing' the Papworth scheme.

He did not elaborate.

This confirmed my view that Treasury would keep the option of 'Papworth to Peterborough' on the table for as long as they wished. Despite the nice words coming from health ministers, saying they had done all that they could to expedite our move to Cambridge, John Wallwork and I were left in no doubt that we had to get the Peterborough option off the table once and for all if our move to Cambridge was to survive.

Following the meeting, John Wallwork wasted no time in briefing Sir Leszek Borysiewicz, the vice chancellor, who was about to attend the Global Economic Forum at Davos, where he had secured a session with George Osborne. Borys, as he was called by close colleagues, also promised to speak with senior officials at Treasury and convey the same message, emphasising yet again the importance of the Cambridge Biomedical Campus to the UK life sciences agenda, and that Papworth Hospital was an important part of that picture.

In the first week of February I was telephoned by Denis Campbell, health reporter at *The Guardian* newspaper. He had interviewed Keith McNeil, the CEO at Cambridge University Hospitals, in preparation for a profile on doctors who had become CEOs. Keith, an Australian, had been a consultant physician in transplantation at Papworth between 1995–2001, and stated how important it was for the Papworth move to be finalised. He alluded to the serious delays that our project was experiencing which, he feared, if not resolved soon, could kill the project.

Denis Campbell then contacted me and asked if I would be prepared to elaborate on these claims.

I had no hesitation in agreeing to his request.

The resulting interview appeared in the Saturday edition of *The Guardian* on 14th February.

The article generated some supportive letters in that paper a few days later from Sir Terence English and

Papworth's future put at risk by Treasury's intervention

Stephen Bridge, chief executive of Papworth, said his hospital was at risk of becoming a casualty of NHS politics

Frank Wells, amongst others. Equally, I received a couple of telephone calls questioning whether it was wise to criticise Treasury.

However, my judgement was that Papworth had behaved impeccably for the 10 long years since our scheme was launched, and despite this, it was in real danger of being killed off for superficial financial reasons, which would make little difference to clearing the significant debt in the Peterborough health economy.

Of course, I was being naïve, but my career was behind me, and I believed it was the right time to stand up and fight for what I believed in.

Two weeks later, a second meeting was convened by Richard Douglas, again at Richmond House, attended by the same representatives from Monitor and Treasury. The atmosphere was tense and, after a few introductory words from Richard Douglas, he admonished me for *The Guardian* interview, whilst Matthew Style just glowered at me across the table.

After this understandable piece of theatre, we got down to business.

Miranda and Martin, from Monitor, spelt out their concerns regarding affordability, and suggested that our patient activity projections should be checked by an independent clinical source. Although they had been verified three times by independent sources (the Department's own heart directors' team, the former SHA and Deloitte), I was happy to support this proposal, confident that our projections were based on expert clinical advice.

Miranda went on to say that Monitor had now spoken with Sir Bruce Keogh, the medical director at NHS England, and a renowned cardiothoracic surgeon. Sir Bruce had provided the names of two doctors who he felt were well qualified to assess both the patient activity projections, and the merits of the Cambridge and Peterborough options.

The meeting finished on good terms, and John Wallwork and I returned to Papworth quietly confident that we could now see light at the end of this very long tunnel.

A few days later I received a telephone call from the person who was to lead the external clinical review. His name was Professor Terence Lewis, and he had recently retired as a cardiothoracic surgeon at Derriford Hospital in Plymouth, where he had moved from London in the mid-1990s to set up a new cardiac centre.

Professor Lewis explained his planned modus operandi, and asked that he and his colleague Professor Tony Davison, a respiratory physician and respiratory lead for the east of England, interview several clinicians from Addenbrooke's, Peterborough and Papworth, as well as commissioners and key figures at NHS England and the University of Cambridge.

The two professors went on to carry out their assignment with great efficiency, interviewing over 40 colleagues from the above named organisations over a two-week period. They produced their findings by the first week of April.

Their report was admirably concise – 11 pages – and free of jargon. It demolished the arguments for moving Papworth to Peterborough, and urged those responsible to make a swift decision to enable the move to the Cambridge Biomedical Campus to finally happen. The report's conclusion was as follows:

> *"This review recommends on clinical grounds the relocation of Papworth to the Cambridge Biomedical Campus with the decision, in principle, being made as a matter of urgency in the interests of patients and for the enhancement of clinical excellence. There is no clinical case for the wholesale or departmental relocation of Papworth to Peterborough."*

In mid-April we heard that George Osborne would be visiting Cambridge the following week to give a speech extolling the virtues of the life sciences sector in this region, and also to announce the go-ahead for a replacement ship for the British Antarctic Survey Organisation, based at the University of Cambridge.

Kate Lancaster, our communications director, John Wallwork and I swung into action and contacted Julian Huppert and asked him to speak to Danny Alexander or, failing that, his political adviser. We wanted to get a sentence inserted into Mr Osborne's speech, supporting the move of Papworth to Cambridge.

A few days later, and the day before the speech, Julian contacted us and said he was quietly confident that a positive comment about the Papworth move to Cambridge would be included in George Osborne's delivery.

The next day, I received three text messages from business acquaintances who were in the audience when George Osborne spoke, congratulating me on getting the final go-ahead for the move to Cambridge. Whilst delighted at the mini-coup we had pulled off, I knew that further details had to be thrashed out with Treasury, and their formidable representative, Matthew Styles.

Five days later, on Tuesday 29th April, my prophecy came true when, at 8.30am, arriving in Huntingdon for the chairs and CEO summit for the Cambridgeshire and Peterborough health economy, I took a call from Matthew.

I half expected to be chastised for getting the sentence inserted in George Osborne's speech, but if that was on his mind, he kept it to himself. Instead he told me there were two sticking points that must be resolved before Treasury ministers could sign off our move to Cambridge.

The first point was that the Papworth board needed to issue a statement agreeing to a merger with Cambridge University Hospitals, and a timescale for achieving that.

The second point was that the Cambridge University Hospitals board was required to give an undertaking to take over the PFI contract in the event that Papworth could not continue to make the payments.

Matthew said that these two points needed to be agreed that day or, at the latest, by the end of the next working day. I reminded him that Papworth had only got this far because the organisations with statutory powers to approve our move to Cambridge only did so on the express intent that Papworth maintained its separate identity and did not merge with Cambridge University Hospitals. These included the Overview and Scrutiny Committees of eight local authorities across East Anglia, and nearly all of the main NHS purchasing health bodies, the primary care trusts, and their successor bodies, the Clinical Commissioning Groups.

I suggested to Matthew that the boards of Papworth and Cambridge University Hospitals would be more than happy to set out those areas where further collaboration, including full integration, was under active consideration.

Later that morning, Keith McNeil spent over an hour on the phone to Matthew confirming what I had said two hours earlier, and I believe that Keith's contribution went a very long way in persuading Matthew to soften his position on this first point.

With regard to the second point, the chair of CUH, Jane Ramsay, conveyed the realpolitik to Matthew, saying that such a proposal would need much longer than the 24 hours he was demanding to get approval from her board and Council of Governors.

Matthew said he would consider what we had told him, but hoped we could still move closer to his position on these two points.

The event which we were attending was the launch of what would become the Sustainability and Transformation Programme (STP) for Cambridgeshire and Peterborough. It finished at 3pm, and we all set off for our various destinations. En route to Papworth, I received an urgent message from Kate Lancaster, telling me that the Treasury's press office had contacted her to discuss the wording of a press release which they hoped to release the following morning, but only if we could reach agreement on the two points.

We contacted Keith and Jane, who were almost back in Cambridge, and asked if they could come to Papworth straightaway. We gathered in John Wallwork's office and drafted some alternative words, which we hoped the Treasury would find acceptable.

Over the next two hours the five of us sent, and responded to, several drafts of the section concerning the two sticking points.

The following day, Wednesday 30th April, saw more exchanges of text, until finally, at 4.19pm, we received an email from the Treasury, which still looked as if Matthew was digging his heels in and refusing to budge from his previous position.

The email sent by a colleague of Matthew's was entitled 'Help'. It read as follows:

"Kate,

How close can you get to accommodating the following in your form of words?

- *Crucial that they start the merger process, i.e. hold board meetings to agree to start the process more or less immediately, i.e. before the deal is formally signed and;*
- *In addition, CUH commits to work with Papworth to mitigate in full any downside scenario that may evolve, including financial support, e.g. will use the hospital capacity if for some reason there is a reduction in demand for Papworth specific services."*

Thirty-five minutes later, following further consultation with Jane Ramsey and Keith McNeil at CUH, we replied as follows:

> *"We propose that the first point reads – The respective CEOs and their senior teams have also been in active discussion since 2013 to identify areas for greater co-operation between our two hospitals, and once the move of Papworth Hospital has been formally signed off we will convene a joint meeting of the two boards of directors to discuss strategic collaboration."*

For the second point we suggested the following wording:

> *"In addition CUH commits to work with Papworth to mitigate any downside scenario that*

> *may evolve, e.g. will use the hospital capacity, if for some reason there is a reduction in demand for Papworth specific services."*

All we could do now was wait.

The next day, Thursday 1st May, was our scheduled Papworth board meeting. At 8.30am I took a call from Matthew Style, who said he wished to convey three things. First, he told me that his ministers had agreed to allow our PFI scheme, for the move to Cambridge to proceed to Financial Close.

Second, Papworth could not proceed to the next, i.e. final stage, the confirmatory business case, until the Department of Health had issued me with a letter containing the conditions underpinning this approval.

His third point was a complete surprise. He thanked me for my courtesy and good manners in what, he acknowledged, were difficult circumstances, and wished me well in the final stage of the project.

I walked to the board meeting with a spring in my step, and hoped the rest of the project would now be plain sailing. One hour into the meeting, John Wallwork left the room to take an urgent phone call. Upon his return, and with a grin as wide as the Cheshire Cat – apt, as George Osborne's constituency was Tatton, Cheshire – John informed the board that the Treasury had just issued a press release concerning our scheme, and he proceeded to read it out loud:

"New hospital to be built in Cambridge.

A £165 million deal for a new hospital has been approved by the Chief Secretary to the Treasury, Danny Alexander, and the Chancellor of the Exchequer, George Osborne, today.

Papworth Hospital, a leading specialist heart and lung hospital, will move from its current location outside Cambridge onto the Addenbrooke's Hospital site in the city. New buildings and facilities will be constructed on the site of the Cambridge Biomedical Campus to accommodate the relocated Papworth Hospital. Papworth Hospital's future location is now secure following years of uncertainty.

The existing buildings at Papworth are over 75 years old. Moving to brand-new purpose-built facilities will ensure the hospital continues to provide world-class medical care and treatment. The proposed new 310-bed Papworth Hospital could boast the latest medical facilities and technologies.

Bringing together two great NHS institutions on the site of the Cambridge Biomedical Campus will also create a hub of world-leading medicine, research and pharmaceutical development. Backing successful research clusters such as this are a key component of our long-term plan for science."

We naturally assumed that the next stage would kick in immediately. However, our colleagues at the Department of Health PFI unit worked at a different pace.

I pressed them for a draft of the Department's approval letter.

Their response was to request that our project director, Ken Brewer, and I attend a meeting with them in London which, we were led to believe, was to go through some of the detail that would be included in this important letter. At this meeting we were told that the letter could not be issued until we provided more information as to why we were planning to appoint Skanska, and not Bouygues, as preferred bidder, as the latter's bid was cheaper.

I was furious, and conveyed that in no uncertain terms. Had they told us this was the real purpose of the meeting, then I would have asked Papworth's medical and nursing directors to accompany us, as they had all the information that the Department of Health required.

It only took us a couple of days to compile a detailed report setting out the clinical reasons which underpinned our decision to award Skanska the contract, which we sent to the Department of Health's officials.

We received a telephone call from the Department within 48 hours, telling us it was all in order, and they fully understood and accepted why Skanska had been selected.

Over the next couple of weeks several drafts of the Department of Health approval letter were sent to me, and then withdrawn, due to errors in detail.

Eventually, on 2nd July, we received the final version of the approval letter, containing 12 conditions which, if breached, would nullify the government's support for our scheme.

The most important of the 12 conditions were:

- The boards of Papworth and Cambridge University hospitals make significant progress with regard to their discussions on strategic collaboration and integration by August, and that the trusts provide a paper at this stage demonstrating that both high-level integration plans and the capital build appear affordable and deliverable within a reasonable timescale.
- That Monitor reviews the affordability again at confirmatory business case stage to provide independent confirmation of an improvement in affordability risk for the scheme.
- That there would need to be further confirmation from commissioners (both central for specialist commissioning and local teams) of the trust's projections of activity, pricing and service configuration (the DH will seek the central confirmation).
- That the DH does not expect any capital cost increases against this total and therefore no revenue cost increases. The unitary payment must remain affordable to the trust and the above requirements for further demonstration

of revenue affordability should by themselves limit any capital cost increases. However, the DH has, in line with its normal practice, set capital and revenue cost caps beyond which the DH's approval would lapse and the business case would need to be reapproved by the DH.

- The trust will ensure that a competition is held to determine the provider of senior debt funding for the scheme.
- Financial Close must be achieved by the end of June 2015.

Although the letter stated we had 12 months to achieve Financial Close, in reality it was only nine months, as the period of purdah would come into force on 1st April 2015, prior to the General Election that had to take place six weeks later.

With the six months needed for achieving final planning consent from Cambridge City Council, there was only a three-month period to conclude all the other matters necessary to achieve Financial Close.

Monitor told us how they planned to carry out their next Affordability Review, scheduled for September. They intended to take a report to their executive committee, scheduled to take place on 11th December. Subject to achieving another satisfactory risk rating from Monitor, and getting final planning consent from Cambridge City Council, on 8th December we would then be on the home straight, with Financial Close, and hence, building work starting only a few weeks away.

Another one of our key tasks was to obtain funding from the Department of Health for those elements that fell outside of the PFI envelope. This included the purchase of eight acres of land at the Cambridge Biomedical Campus from the commercial developers, and the taking out of low-interest loans to cover 44% of the building and equipment costs. Despite our frustration with the Department of Health over the many delays our project had suffered, they were very helpful in putting in place a most favourable financial package.

Our scheme was shaping up to have one of the best funding packages the NHS had put in place for a new hospital project going back almost 20 years.

After all the turbulence of the past, things were falling into place, and my colleagues and I prepared the necessary papers for our board of directors meeting to be held on 27th November. At this meeting we would need to sign the self-certification paperwork, essential to enable Monitor to 'approve' the scheme at their executive committee meeting on 11th December.

At 6pm on Wednesday 26th November, Martin Smith from Monitor rang to tell me that they believed we might have a £7 million black hole in our finances for the next financial year, and that under no circumstances were we to sign the self-certification forms at our board meeting the next morning.

He explained that the proposed changes to the tariff for 'specialised services', proposed by NHS England, would be devastating for Papworth, and deal a killer blow to our scheme. As 70% of Papworth's income came from this source, I was hardly in a position to argue, and the phrase 'Houston, we have a problem' came to mind. We agreed to gather our colleagues together for a teleconference call at 8.30am the next morning.

I went home fearing the worst.

The next morning I gave my apologies to the board, and went ahead with the conference call with Monitor. It concluded some 30 minutes later with me acknowledging that I needed to persuade NHS England to pay more for some of the services they commissioned from Papworth. I reported this to the board, and later that day managed to speak with Dr Paul Watson, the regional director of the Midlands and east for NHS England. Paul was sympathetic but, as expected, gave no ground and said we needed to get our respective experts together to see if we could thrash out a solution.

Over the next week, Papworth's director of finance, Jane Payling, the project accountant, Zoe Selmes, and contracting colleagues, especially Sue Shepherd, whom I had appointed way back in 1990, met on several occasions, and 'pulled the proverbial rabbit out of the hat'. They came up with a series of measures that would reduce the proposed financial gap to a level that could be bridged. We hoped this package would be acceptable to Monitor and allow them to go ahead and provide a risk rating for our PFI scheme. The nub of these proposals centred on those specialised services which were not paid on tariff.

During the frenetic discussions held over this period, it transpired that Papworth was being paid a lower rate than our counterparts at Basildon Cardiothoracic Centre (for critical care), and less for cystic fibrosis, and heart and lung transplants than the Royal Brompton and Harefield NHS trust. The latter had been known to us for many years but not acted upon, given the influential lobbying conducted by most of the major London hospitals.

The result of these negotiations with NHS England, i.e. to pay Papworth the same rate as our counterparts, brought the potential income and expenditure gap for the next financial year down from £7 million to £2 million.

All I had to do now was to get Paul Watson's approval to these proposals.

A date for my meeting with Paul was set, and I arrived at NHS England's regional offices, at Fulbourn, Cambridge, in good time. Whilst waiting in the reception area, I received a phone call from Ken Brewer with some more bad news: Cambridge City Council were thinking of tabling a last-minute condition for our final planning consent, calling on Papworth to give a commitment to underwrite the cost of another multi-storey car park on the Cambridge Biomedical Campus.

Just as I was about to enter one of the most important meetings of my life, I found myself on the phone pleading with the director of planning at Cambridge City Council to accept that as Papworth was one of several tenants on the campus, then any commitment should be shared by all parties. After a long pause he agreed to review the wording of the paper that had been drafted, and would get his officials to agree the detail with Papworth's project director, Ken Brewer.

I then went into my meeting with Paul Watson feeling slightly fazed.

As ever in our dealings, Paul took a pragmatic view, and once he was satisfied that no precedents were being set, or special favours done, then he was happy to sign off the series of revisions our respective colleagues had come up with, to ameliorate the impact of the tariff/NHS specialised services income for Papworth for 2015/16 financial year.

Over the next few days, Ken Brewer resolved the car parking issue with the council, and final planning approval was obtained for new Papworth Hospital on 5th December 2014.

Due to the problem with Papworth's 2015/16 tariff, Monitor said that they could no longer stick with their original timescale to formally consider the outcome of their Affordability Review on 11th December. They were adamant that it would now have to go the following executive committee meeting on 21st January 2015. Nothing I said would budge them; we would just have to sweat it out over the next seven weeks.

Needless to say, Christmas 2014 was not one of my happiest yuletides.

CHAPTER TWENTY-ONE

2015

Snatching Defeat from the Jaws of Victory

In January, the news from Monitor got worse.

Martin Smith told me that given the political sensitivity around Cambridgeshire, they had to be absolutely certain they covered all facets of our scheme, and they were now considering a further delay and thinking about taking the Affordability Review to their 12th February executive committee. If that were to happen, I told Martin, it would mean the death of our scheme. We would have precious little time to complete the other tasks, as the Department of Health approval letter clearly stated they could only happen once Monitor had given us an appropriate risk rating.

I wrote to Monitor expressing my grave concerns:

> *"Should Monitor decide to defer considering the affordability of this move until 12th February, this will add £3 million to the costs, significantly*

unnerve our PFI partner, Skanska, and the funders and almost certainly delay Financial Close till after the General Election.

In reality, that will kill the scheme, wasting millions of pounds of public money."

I then contacted Andrew Lansley's office. He had recently announced that he was standing down as MP, so I hoped he would feel able to get actively involved, and atone for the bombshell he'd dropped almost five years earlier.

Andrew was not around, but his senior parliamentary assistant, Briony, had briefed him on the reason for my visit. She took a copy of my letter to Monitor and said she would draft something appropriate in Andrew's name and email it to George Osborne and Danny Alexander.

A couple of days later Briony sent me the reply Andrew had received from the chancellor and the chief secretary. It read:

"Dear Andrew,

Thank you for your email bringing to our attention the concerns of Stephen Bridge regarding the timing of final approvals for Papworth Hospital's PFI scheme.

We would like to reaffirm our support for the scheme and assure you that Treasury officials are working with the Department of Health on an approvals timetable which would allow Papworth to complete the PFI deal before the end of February, subject to expected approval by the Monitor board. This would avoid the two issues which Stephen Bridge notes in his email, namely that a delay would result in increased scheme costs and risk the approvals process running into purdah.

We are very happy for our officials to discuss this with Stephen Bridge directly. We hope this is sufficient to allay your, and Papworth's concerns.

George Osborne, Danny Alexander."

This was very reassuring, and I immediately went to Andrew Lansley's office and gave Briony a large bouquet of flowers to thank her for taking the initiative and drafting the email on behalf of Andrew Lansley.

Martin Smith contacted me the next day and said the main reason for Monitor's extreme caution was the lack of a detailed letter of support from NHS England. Four drafts had been discussed by these two organisations and finally the deadlock was broken and a fifth – and thankfully, final – draft was sent by NHS England's Midlands and east regional office and duly accepted by Monitor on 23rd January.

Martin Smith kindly rang me that evening to tell me that they were now in a position to formally consider our scheme at their executive committee meeting on 30th January.

Following their deliberations, Monitor issued Papworth with a final transaction risk of 'amber', sufficient for us to proceed to Financial Close. This rating was fair, given the recent scare over the tariff for specialised services.

Monitor's letter to us spelt out the risks that we both acknowledged, and concluded by stating: "*However, none of the issues identified are sufficiently serious to stop or delay the transaction.*"

We entered February hoping to achieve Financial Close by the end of that month. The NHS PFI rules required a final approval letter from the Department of Health. In spite of many reassuring noises during our numerous telephone calls with officials, their letter did not arrive.

Then, true to form, the bad luck that had dogged this project over the years, struck again. The date was Friday 13th February . . .

Ken Brewer came to my office and told me that Skanska were asking for more money, or else they might pull out.

The succession of delays had meant they had incurred significant extra costs, and despite what the PFI rulebook said about the private sector party shouldering the risks, I was naturally very concerned that the scheme might falter and die at one minute before midnight.

I knew that we were going to have to play a game of poker, but there was no alternative.

The following week, Ken and I met with the two most senior people in Skanska UK, who, as the script demanded, 'laid it on with a trowel'. The cost of labour in

Cambridge, the poor ground conditions, the delay with (and poor quality of) the haulage road into the site, all added up to financial cost, way above their successful bid.

As the saying goes 'we were between a rock and a hard place'.

Department of Health approval would lapse if our scheme exceeded a capital cost of £million[8]. Suspecting that Skanska were not bluffing, and recalling their words 'it is not too late for us to walk away', we needed to find a solution.

Skanska said that a decision would be made at their next UK board meeting, due to be held the following week, which would be chaired by their global CEO, flying in from Sweden, to consider the status of their main UK projects.

Although rumours abounded that Skanska had won the contract to build the two Astra Zeneca buildings on the Cambridge Biomedical Campus, I did not feel inclined to call their bluff.

With NHS finances in such a parlous state and getting worse, this would be the last chance for a decade – possibly much, much longer – to build a new Papworth Hospital in Cambridge.

Over the next few days, Ken Brewer, Jane Payling and Zoe Selmes crunched the numbers to see if some items could be moved from pre- to post-contract, so as not to breach the capital limit set by the Department of

---

8 Figure withheld for reasons of confidentiality.

Health. We hoped this would give Skanska UK some wriggle room, and perhaps allow their UK executives to show their global CEO that they had driven a hard bargain with us.

In this surreal and nerve-wracking week, the Department of Health finally issued us with their final approval letter, on 19th February. Upon reading it, they stipulated that Financial Close must take place by the end of February. Due to the last-minute concerns raised by Skanska, this would not now be possible.

We decided not to ask the Department for a revised letter until we knew that the problems with Skanska had been resolved, and that we still had a scheme to close.

On Friday 20th February we sent our financial proposals to Skanska, ready for their board meeting early the following week . . . and held our breath.

Late afternoon on Tuesday 24th February, I took a phone call from the Skanska UK boss who told me that our financial package had been accepted and approved at their board meeting and, as far as they were concerned, it was now 'all systems go'. He then asked if their global CEO could come to Papworth the next day to meet with me and my senior colleagues.

The next morning the Skanska team met with John Wallwork, Ken Brewer and myself, and we celebrated over a cup of coffee, and conversed as if the drama of the last few weeks had never happened. A good omen was that the revised Department of Health final approval letter was emailed to me during this meeting.

Negotiations with the (mainly European) bank's funding 56% of the scheme's costs went well, and our legal and financial advisers (Bevan Britten and KPMG, respectively) felt that everything should be in place to achieve Financial Close in the first week of March or, at the latest, the second week.

To be on the safe side, it was agreed that the second week of March was the more prudent, and Wednesday 11th was earmarked for this final act before construction work on the new Papworth Hospital could begin.

When the day arrived, Ken Brewer, Jane Payling, Zoe Selmes and I arrived at the offices of Skanska's legal advisers in the City of London, ready to 'seal the deal'.

Upon entering the large boardroom, the impression I got was that we were now going to act out a piece of theatre, presumably commonplace in the world of big business.

There were approximately 30 lawyers and accountants darting in and out of the various side rooms, checking and rechecking the documentation, whilst the four of us from Papworth looked on, talking amongst ourselves for at least three hours, as we were informed they would call us when it was our time to perform.

It turned out to be a long day, as the advisers continued their conversations and added document after document, laid out in piles on the huge board room table, at least four metres square. There must have been five hundred documents, with coloured sheets of red, amber and green on top of each pile. A successful outcome would be for all the piles to have turned from red to green by the end of the working day, which was 3pm in London, and 4pm in Luxembourg, the headquarters of the main European bank.

As the clock turned 2pm, we were told that it was unlikely that the deal could be closed that day, but it would be in order for Jane Payling and I to sign the documents ready for Financial Close to happen the following day.

So, at 4pm, Jane and I commenced signing the documents, and after one hour our work was done, and the boardroom table was a sea of green papers.

I was told I did not need to be there the next day, so the four of us left the building and headed for Kings Cross Station, slightly bemused at the day's events.

Jane and Ken returned to London on Thursday 12th March, promising to keep me informed of progress. It was difficult to concentrate on normal business at Papworth and, true to form, Jane rang me at 10am to tell me a problem had arisen. The boss of the main European bank funding our scheme was in Scotland, where he was closing a deal for a project in Dumfries. The advisers did not want to risk asking his deputy to close our deal, so the only solution was to wait for this executive's aeroplane to arrive back in Luxembourg.

I could not help thinking that our project was jinxed, and feared that Financial Close might not happen today after all. We had previously been told by our advisers that our deal could not be closed on a Friday, as the markets became jittery as the weekend approached. So failure to seal the deal that day meant that we would have to go into the third week of March, perilously close to the General Election purdah period, entailing a shutdown of major government business, which, given the political heat around PFI schemes, almost certainly included our project.

I concluded that it was now out of our hands. I had always believed in fate, so here was a chance to put that to the test.

Jane Payling rang again at noon to tell me that the European bank executive was due to land at 1.30pm London time, and provided his plane was not delayed, there would be 90 minutes to close this deal before the markets closed for the week.

John Wallwork was understandably anxious, and came to my office at least three times that morning, only for me to say that it was too close to call, so I suggested that he went for another walk.

At 2pm, John appeared in my office for the fourth time, presumably having walked several miles around the hospital grounds and, like me, was very anxious to hear how things were progressing in London.

The next thing, my phone rang, and it was Jane Payling, barely audible above the cheering and popping of champagne corks. "Steve, we've done it! We got there! See you tomorrow!"

So that was it.

Thirteen years after having submitted our first business case for the move to the Cambridge Biomedical Campus, and after countless reviews by the Department of Health, the Treasury and Monitor, and repelling several threats as described above, the move of Papworth Hospital was going to happen, after all.

Not surprisingly, several of my colleagues at Papworth and elsewhere in the NHS did not believe that the move would happen. With all the setbacks, people probably thought that I was 'keeping a brave face' and did not know when to admit defeat; but after the satisfaction of seeing the bulldozers onsite in Cambridge, it was business as usual at Papworth.

We had only just missed out on achieving an 'Outstanding' rating from the Care Quality Commission, following their inspection in December 2014, due mainly to out-of-date risk registers at departmental and ward level. This triggered the usual response from Monitor, who insisted that we spent money on hiring management consultants to review our board governance arrangements, despite having done so only six months earlier. I argued in vain that there should only be a review of the few areas that our previous exercise had not covered, mainly quality governance. We therefore had to spend £40,000 to engage one of the Big Four consultancies, so favoured by Monitor, to repeat the exercise, and which eventually gave us a clean bill of health.

In late summer we were informed that Secretary of State, Jeremy Hunt, would like to visit Papworth. Part of his time was to be spent in a Q&A session with a cross-section of staff, but excluding the presence of hospital managers. I was disappointed with this request, as I had prided myself on maintaining excellent relationships with all staff and believed that there was not an 'us and them' culture at Papworth.

This style of ministerial approach was so different to the way matters were conducted with the many ministers I had personal contact with over the previous 30 years. It felt that my management colleagues and I were being classified as 'guilty until proved innocent', and that Jeremy Hunt was more interested in garnering supportive media headlines than hearing the views of managers at the sharp end.

Although I soon became immersed in my work, I felt that I needed to decide quickly if I was going to retire, or should I see the move through to Cambridge.

As 2015 drew to a close, and I reached the age of 60, I gave a lot of thought to my future . . . And concluded that as I was also approaching 40 years working in the NHS, it was the right time to bow out.

CHAPTER TWENTY-TWO

2016

The Final Curtain

I informed John Wallwork of my decision after the Christmas break, and felt that by stepping down now I would give my successor two years to oversee the complex task of moving Papworth onto the Cambridge Biomedical Campus.

Early the following week, I was told by our recently appointed director of finance that an allegation of fraud had been made against me, but that he was not at liberty to tell me of the nature of the claim. I spent an uncomfortable week waiting until Elizabeth Horne, our director of human resources, returned from leave to inform her of this allegation. Elizabeth received the same answer as I did: that she was not allowed to know the nature of the allegation against me.

It took approximately four weeks before the finance director told me that the allegation had not been proved, and the matter was closed. When I received confirmation in writing, I saw that the allegation was that I had spent a 'considerable sum of money from charitable funds decorating my office'.

I did not know whether to laugh or cry! This allegation could have been investigated and concluded the same day with an inspection of my office, where the desk, two chairs and carpet were 20 years old, the sofa seven years old, and that my swivel chair – the swivel chair! – was the only thing that was fairly new, but had cost less than £100! It was an 'in joke' at Papworth that I was proud of my slightly austere office, decorated only twice in 28 years, so that I was able to say that the overwhelming majority of money was justifiably spent in clinical areas.

This convinced me of the apparent recent change in NHS culture, i.e. the 'guilty until proven innocent' culture where, what should have been a simple, common sense approach, was now replaced by impersonal, legalistic and disrespectful processes. Any doubts that I may have had about retiring were banished from my mind after reflecting on this episode.

As I left Papworth, at the end of March 2016, I felt proud that my management style had left the hospital in good shape, much stronger than when I joined in 1988, and with the clinical staff justifiably proud of the superb care they provide to the many thousands of patients they treat each year.

Over my 28 years at Papworth, the number of patients treated had increased from 7,000 to 107,000 a year, the number of staff employed had grown from 400 to 2,000, and the hospital's annual budget increased from £8 million to £140 million.

Despite the massive increase in NHS red tape over these years, I felt that we maintained the 'can do' ethos that I inherited from the senior medical and nursing staff in 1988; and in the three years since I left Papworth, it is gratifying to see that the hospital is still a leading institution in the NHS.

The start of an exciting new era on the world-class Cambridge Biomedical Campus has now begun, where Papworth will surely thrive for the next 100 years of its existence.

Investment in Major Schemes at Papworth Hospital 1988–2015
Total £36.6 million

	Cost (In £Thousands)
1989 – Surgical Unit, 12-bed extension	330
1990 – Radiology, Gamma camera and room to locate it in	200
1991 – Transplant Outpatients Department	120
1992 – Operating Department, two-storey extension with two theatres	2200
1993 – Varrier-Jones Ward, two storeys comprising 22 beds, lecture theatre, consulting rooms	1600
1993 – Respiratory Support and Sleep Centre, comprising 12 beds	860
1993 – Main reception, including centralised Medical Records Dept.	300
1994 – Cardiac Catheterisation Laboratory	800
1994 – Cystic Fibrosis Unit, comprising 12 beds	300
1995 – CT Scanner and Thoracic Oncology facilities	1200
1995 – Fifth operating theatre	1200
1996 – Cardiology Day Case Unit, comprising 12 beds	600

1997 –	RSSC Extension, eight beds	400
1997 –	Replacement Cardiology and Cardiac Surgery ward block, comprising 45 beds	2200
1998 –	Transplant Outpatient Department and new lecture theatre	1400
1999 –	Histopathology Laboratory	1600
2000 –	Chest Medical Unit, Outpatients extension	400
2001 –	Two-storey building housing 26 ICU beds and 18 Cardiology Day Case beds	5800
2001 –	Cardiac Catheterisation Laboratory – fourth room	1500
2002 –	Research and Development Bio Incubator Building	1600
2003 –	Microbiology Laboratory and Mortuary	1800
2003 –	Princess Ward, Chest Medical Unit, comprising 16 beds	900
2004 –	Respiratory Support and Sleep Centre extension, 12 beds	1200
2004 –	Cardiac Catheterisation Laboratory – fifth room, and Hemingford Ward comprising 12 beds	2300
2005 –	Radiology Diagnostic Unit, including Cardiac MRI and CT scanners	3000
2013 –	Varrier Jones Ward extension comprising 12 beds	2800

The Future of Papworth Hospital: Summary of Key Events

June 1991 – Huntingdon Health Authority recommends that Papworth Hospital should be partially redeveloped on its existing site in Papworth Everard.

September 1991 – East Anglian RHA says that a move to Cambridge should still be an option, and plans to undertake further work to assess that option.

June 1992 – Prime Minister and MP for Huntingdon, John Major, goes public in his support for Papworth Hospital to stay on its Papworth Everard site.

September 1992 – RHA agrees to support a partial redevelopment at Papworth Everard.

April 1994 – RHA disbanded but deployed delaying tactics, before giving Papworth the final go-ahead to redevelop, as it had promised 18 months earlier.

June 1994 – Anglia and Oxford regional office requests further information from Papworth before it says it can grant go-ahead of partial redevelopment.

April 1995 – Prime Minister John Major visits Papworth to open new operating theatre and is shocked to hear that redevelopment of hospital has not started, two and a half years after the decision to support it was given.

October 1995 – Following private correspondence between Stephen Bridge and prime minister's office, regional office gives go-ahead for redevelopment.

January 1996 – Papworth begins the Private Finance Initiative (PFI) process with a briefing event for potential bidders.

October 1996 – Design of redevelopment awarded to Sir Robert McAlpine Ltd, a major construction company.

June 1997 – New government of Tony Blair halts all NHS PFI schemes.

July 1997 – Papworth scheme cancelled.

April 1999 – Cambridgeshire Health Authority launches blueprint for changes to the NHS in that county for the next 25 years, including the move of Papworth Hospital to a site adjacent to Addenbrooke's Hospital.

January 2002 – Papworth submits business case to regional office for a move to Cambridge.

February 2002 – Regional office tells Papworth that we will have to wait until the Department of Health requests bids for major capital schemes to be submitted.

January 2004 – Department of Health issues request for submission of major capital schemes. Papworth's is one of 13 to be received by the Department.

July 2004 – All 13 schemes are allowed to continue to the second stage of the three-stage process.

February 2006 – Papworth's scheme passes the first independent check of its all-round robustness.

August 2007 – Papworth's scheme is halted when the Strategic Health Authority and the regulator of foundation trusts, an organisation called Monitor, withdraw their support in favour of an alternative proposal suggested by Addenbrooke's, now rebranded as Cambridge University Hospitals, which they claim is £30 million cheaper than Papworth's own scheme.

December 2007 – Cambridge University Hospitals acknowledge that their proposal is not cheaper, accepting Papworth's detailed evidence which shows their scheme offers the best value for money to the taxpayer.

July 2008 – Monitor carries out first Affordability Review of scheme. We pass, so project continues.

November 2008 – Papworth's scheme passes the second independent check of its all-round robustness.

December 2008 – SHA confirms its support for Papworth's outline business case (OBC), i.e. stage two out of three-stage process.

December 2009 – Monitor carries out second Affordability Review. We pass, so project continues.

April 2010 – OBC, i.e. stage two, approved by Department of Health on day before Good Friday. However, on day after Easter Monday, Prime Minister Gordon Brown calls a General Election, so Papworth scheme is halted until the new government is in place.

August 2010 – Department of Health allows Papworth scheme to proceed to next stage. As PFI process has been updated, number of stages has been increased from three to seven. Papworth enters stage three and advertises in *European Journal*, then selects three companies to prepare proposals.

November 2011 – Papworth selects best two bids to go forward to stage four.

April 2012 – Monitor carries out third Affordability Review. Papworth passes.

July 2012 – Papworth scheme passes the third independent check of its all-round robustness.

April 2013 – Monitor carries out fourth Affordability Review. Papworth passes.

June 2013 – The government, specifically the Treasury, launches a rescue plan for the Peterborough Hospital PFI, and insists that Papworth's scheme must be halted until proposals for Peterborough's future are known, even if that means forcing Papworth to move to Peterborough and not Cambridge.

February 2014 – Papworth's CEO, Stephen Bridge, goes public, with an interview in *The Guardian* newspaper to criticise the Treasury and their support to force Papworth to move to Peterborough.

March 2014 – Monitor carries out fifth Affordability Review. Papworth passes.

April 2014 – Chancellor of the Exchequer, George Osborne, gives a speech in Cambridge giving support, in principle, to Papworth's move to the Cambridge Biomedical Campus. This came about through initiative from Cambridge Liberal Democrat MP Julian Huppert's contacts with Liberal Democrat deputy to the chancellor, Danny Alexander, as part of the Coalition Government.

May 2014 – Treasury officials give draft approval to Papworth, entering penultimate stage, stage six, of process.

June 2014 – Treasury officials give approval to Papworth to enter seventh and final stage.

November 2014 – Monitor inform Papworth that initial findings of next year's NHS tariff, i.e. income for treating patients, looks like the scheme will be unaffordable.

December 2014 – Papworth and NHS England agree a financial settlement, which returns scheme to viability.

January 2015 – Monitor carries out sixth Affordability Review. Papworth passes.

February 2015 – Skanska, the company hired to build new Papworth Hospital, threaten to pull out unless they can obtain better financial terms. Papworth agrees to transfer some of the money held in reserve to give them assurance they are seeking for their board in Sweden.

March 2015 – Financial Close reached, European banks sign off deal, enabling building work to commence straightaway.

May 2019 – New Papworth Hospital opens and treats its first patients.